DEBATING EDUCATION

DEBATING ETHICS

General Editor
Christopher Heath Wellman
Washington University St. Louis

Debating Ethics is a series of volumes in which leading scholars defend opposing views on timely ethical questions and core theoretical issues in contemporary moral, political, and legal philosophy.

Debating Education

Is There a Role for Markets?

DAVID SCHMIDTZ AND

HARRY BRIGHOUSE

OXFORD
UNIVERSITY PRESS

OXFORD

UNIVERSITY PRESS

Oxford University Press is a department of the University of Oxford. It furthers
the University's objective of excellence in research, scholarship, and education
by publishing worldwide. Oxford is a registered trade mark of Oxford University
Press in the UK and certain other countries.

Published in the United States of America by Oxford University Press
198 Madison Avenue, New York, NY 10016, United States of America.

© Oxford University Press 2020

CIP data is on file at the Library of Congress
ISBN 978-0-19-930095-2 (pbk.)
ISBN 978-0-19-930094-5 (hbk.)

1 3 5 7 9 8 6 4 2

Paperback printed by LSC Communications, United States of America
Hardback printed by Bridgeport National Bindery, Inc., United States of America

My parents learned to read and write in the 1920s. Then, after the sixth grade, they went back to work on their family farms. Their six children—my generation—were the first generation to attend high school. Four of us graduated; three of us went on to attend college, and two of us graduated from that. My brother Jim got a degree in education and became a schoolteacher.

My father was not a worldly man, but he said something I never forgot. I had just turned eighteen. He was helping me to move to a place of my own, a room in a basement a few miles away. We had been fighting, which was part of why I felt I had to move. Dad had little to say that day, as usual, but as the last box was unloaded and we sat in his car, waiting for me to get out, close the door on my childhood, and get on with my life, Dad said, "Make sure you're worth more than they pay you."

Having had to sell our farm six years earlier (160 acres was too small to compete with emerging economies of scale of agribusiness), Dad became a janitor and weekend bartender. That was all he would ever be. Yet when I entered the building where he worked and went to his floor, I was walking down hallways that were clean. *Make sure you're worth more than they pay you.* I was a teenager. It had been years since I had been a good listener. But I listened to that.

People migrate around the globe to give their children a shot at a better life. One of our highest aspirations: to produce a next generation that will be better than us. If you are taught by a farmer father, the best you can be is a forewarned farmer. If you go to city school—taught by adults who work full-time to gather and pass on information about a world of "what if"—your ceiling rises. Our job as educators is to position students to be something their parents were not. Our job is to enable them to be themselves, and to make real whatever latent excellence they have within them. We need to offer our students a better product than they've ever been offered before.

Or die trying. That's where the fun is.
—David Schmidtz, Tucson, Arizona

CONTENTS

PART II DEBATING MARKETS IN EDUCATION

Harry Brighouse

PREFACE

When Kit Wellman asked me to do a volume in his new Debating Ethics series, I said I'd debate markets in education if I could recruit Harry Brighouse to be my partner. Kit was intrigued. He had no idea I was interested in the topic. I said education is among the most compelling practical challenges of our time. And while several philosophers are doing admirable work in the area, Brighouse is in a class by himself. The difference between a clever philosopher and a great one boils down to honesty. Brighouse is honest. He was the one from whom I had the most to learn.

Knowing Harry's work, I expect that much of what he says will turn out to be true, important, and illuminating. This book takes the form of a debate, but in any case I recruited Harry to be my partner in this debate precisely because I would not bet against him. He wants the best for his children and yours. He wants to know what works. When Harry and I first met, we were graduate students in our twenties. We both knew in our bones that philosophy is not a team sport, and at its best philosophy is not about winning. We are after the truth. There is nothing I'd rather do than get after it together.

This essay concerns markets in education generally, not education at a particular age or grade level. Some of my remarks pertain to colleges, others to early childhood education. Unless I specify otherwise, or the context makes it obvious, I am envisioning issues as they arise in high schools, without supposing the problems are unique to high schools.

My work was supported by a grant from the John Templeton Foundation. The opinions expressed here are mine and do not necessarily reflect the views of the Templeton Foundation. Over the years, aside from what I have learned from Harry, I've learned from conversations with Loren Lomasky and Susan Moller Okin, with an audience at Stanford, with members of all my seminars, and with Ralf Bader, Neera Badhwar, Sameer Bajaj, Pete Boettke, Jason Brennan, Matt Brown, Allen Buchanan, Tom Christiano, Matthew Clayton, Bill Galston, Stefanie Haeffele-Balch, John Hasnas, Bobbi Herzberg, Cate Johnson, Bill Kline, Jayme Lemke, Andy Mason, Dan Moller, Carmen Pavel, Mark Pennington, Fabienne Peter, Massimo Renzo, Debra Satz, Danny Shahar, Emily Skarbek, Stephen Stich, Virgil Storr, Adam Swift, Hannah Tierney, Adam Swift, Chad Van Schoelandt, and Dick Wagner.

I'm also grateful to the Earhart Foundation for support in the fall of 2013, and to Ed Eisele for supporting Robert Lusch, Cate Johnson, and me when we were writing *Ethics, Economy, and Entrepreneurship* and were needing to rethink everything we thought we knew about teaching. My thanks also to the Georgetown Institute for the Study of

Markets and Ethics for hosting a workshop on a draft of the manuscript (and for hosting me as visiting professor) in the fall of 2016, and to George Mason University's F. A. Hayek Program for Advanced Study in Philosophy, Politics, and Economics, and King's College London's Department of Political Economy for providing an excellent working environment over the years.

Finally, I thank Randy and Ken Kendrick. In 2003, when it seemed I would die (or worse) from a brain tumor, I met Randy at a formal dinner. She saw something in me that inspired her to find out what could be done and who could do it. Because of Randy and the one-of-a-kind surgeon she found, Robert Spetzler, I am here, still working, and still waking up every morning knowing that, compared to that experience, the day ahead will be a piece of cake.

—**David Schmidtz, Tucson, Arizona, 2018**

When David invited me to join him in this project, I was enthusiastic. Despite the fact that we have quite different views about many issues in political philosophy—or maybe because of it—I've learned a good deal from David's work over the years, and I hoped that what I was sure would turn out to be disagreements about markets in education would be productive. My main hesitation was that perhaps we would not disagree enough to make for a sharp debate. Both of us approach philosophy—and politics—in a spirit of comradely deliberation, and neither of us is a natural controversialist. Over the course of the project, as I anticipated, we have discovered points of agreement. But, fortunately for the project and for the reader, a good deal of disagreement remains.

My thinking about education as revealed here is indebted to many. Foremost among them are my frequent collaborator Adam Swift; my dad, Tim Brighouse; and my wife, Lynn Glueck. Many of my philosophical ideas about compulsory education have been formulated with or adjusted through conversation with Adam, and some of my ideas are just his. For my ideas about policy, the same is true of Tim; for my ideas about practice, the same is true of Lynn. And each has also influenced me in categories of thinking that they are not primarily responsible for! So although nobody but me has responsibility for any of my errors, if anybody else did have responsibility (which they don't), it would be them. Mike McPherson, Jennifer Jennings, Susanna Loeb, Helen "Sunny" Ladd, and Gina Schouten have all exerted considerable influence as well, although, again, they are not responsible for any of the errors. Chapter 2 of my contribution draws on ideas from *Educational Goods*, a book I recently co-authored with Adam, Susanna, and Sunny. I take full responsibility for any errors there, too. I'm indebted to many other people for influencing my contribution to the book, and the debts cover so many years that I can only mention some here: Jaime Ahlberg, Deborah Lowenberg Ball, Chris Bertram, Samuel Bowles, Randall Curren, Kyla Ebels-Duggan, William Galston, Herbert Gintis, Daniel Hausman, Diana Hess, Sandy Jencks, Tony Laden, Paula McAvoy, Jennifer Morton, Jennifer Noyes, David O'Brien, Sally Power, John Roemer, Elaine Unterhalter, John White, Geoff Whitty, Daniel Wikler, John Witte, and Erik Wright. Thanks, too, to Kailey Mullane for editorial help at the end of the project. And we're both grateful to Grace Gecewicz for compiling the index.

—Harry Brighouse, Madison, Wisconsin, 2018

DEBATING EDUCATION

Introduction

HARRY BRIGHOUSE AND DAVID SCHMIDTZ

SINCE THE LATE 1980S TWO kinds of reform have dominated education policy in the English-speaking world. Standards-based reforms have established curricular standards that all government schools (and, in some countries, even private schools) must abide by. For example, until 1988 the UK government required only two compulsory subjects in schools in England and Wales: physical education and religious education. The 1988 Education Act established curricular standards for English, mathematics, languages, the social sciences, and the natural sciences for all age levels. Until the early 1990s most US states had no statewide guidance on curriculum; by 2016 most states had detailed Common Core standards for mathematics and English language arts, and most had some standards for the full range of other subjects.

Market-based reforms spread the ideas that schools should compete with one another and that parents should have more power to select what school their child attends. The 1981 Education Act for England and Wales established that local authorities must take account of parental preference when allocating children to schools; after the 1988 Education Act a full-blown school choice system emerged.

Now all parents must rank-order several schools, and those preferences play a substantial role in determining where children attend. Starting in the 1970s many large US cities have had magnet schools, which harness parental choice, usually to promote racial integration. In the early 1990s, though, two major reforms were introduced. Wisconsin established a voucher school system in Milwaukee, through which low-income parents could opt out of traditional public schools and the state would pay for their children to attend eligible private schools. Minnesota and California passed charter school legislation, establishing schools that are less strictly regulated than traditional public schools and which children attend on the basis of choice (when the schools have more applicants than they have room for, they must select by lottery). Voucher programs currently operate in several cities, and forty-three states and the District of Columbia have charter school legislation. This book is primarily about the market reforms, although from time to time we do touch on issues raised by standards-based reform.

The intellectual case for market-based reform was made forcefully by the classical liberal economist Milton Friedman as early as 1956. He suggested that the defenders of government provision of schooling were conflating three functions: funding, regulation, and provision. He argued that there was a strong case, grounded in the public interest in education, for the government to ensure some amount of funding for every child to attend school but that this case had no bearing on how the government should regulate schooling or whether it should provide schooling. He believed that government provision was unresponsive to the interests of parents: if your child effectively has to attend a particular school, and if that school will receive funds for the child no matter what you do, then the school has no incentive to listen to any complaints or suggestions you might have. If, on the other hand, schools were independent organizations that had to compete for students (and the financial resources that accompany them), they would be more responsive.

Although the intellectual case for market reforms in general came from the political right, the specific idea of charter schools was developed on the political left. Friedman imagined the government completely withdrawing from the provision of schooling and adopting a regulatory framework that had no special curricular aspects; the government would provide a voucher for each child, and private providers would compete on an open market. But Albert Shanker, the longtime leader of the American Federation of Teachers, made a different proposal. Most of the school system should stay more or less as it was, but groups of parents or teachers, or members of the community, could establish small schools of choice, funded by the government but operating under much looser regulations than the traditional schools with which they would coexist. This would enable the system to harness the efforts of teachers and parents whose talents and inclinations are not efficiently used in the heavily bureaucratic traditional system. Shanker envisioned charters as crucibles of innovation and experimentation, potentially developing better ideas and better practices that could be emulated throughout the system.

Voucher programs have, very partially, implemented Friedman's vision; in some states charter schools are used roughly as Shanker envisioned, whereas in others they resemble Friedman's vision. But in most places in the United States, both innovations operate alongside more traditional arrangements. In England, by contrast, the whole system now resembles a kind of compromise between the two visions: almost all schools are effectively charter schools, but they operate under quite detailed curricular regulations.

Markets have always been part of the way schooling is organized. What Americans call public schooling emerged only in the nineteenth century, and in Britain it was only in 1944 that the patchwork of arrangements through which most children attended school until the age of thirteen was formalized into a system in which the government directly funded most schools. Even then, most elementary education continued to be provided by religious schools, and although students were usually assigned to a default neighborhood school, parents could always opt for a school that better matched their religious commitment. And in both countries a thriving private school sector operated in the background: any family with the resources could opt out of the public schools into the private sector. When it comes to providing schooling, reform did not introduce markets; it extended them.

Both public and academic debates about market reforms consistently raise philosophical questions, which are often left unexplored even though addressing them is essential to making progress in those debates. These include, but are not limited to, the following:

What counts as a good educational outcome for children? When someone says reform will improve outcomes, they typically have some set of outcomes in mind. Recent accountability reforms in the United States have tended to measure outcomes just in terms of performance on mathematics and reading tests, but even enthusiasts of those reforms believe that other educational goods matter profoundly. A recent study shows that the state of California expects a wide-ranging and complex set of educational outcomes for all children. In Britain, until 1988 the government set no outcomes-related expectations at all.[1]

What counts as a good distributive outcome? One might think that everyone should, ideally, have a similar level of educational success; another ideal might be that resources be provided to optimize talent development; yet another might be that inequalities in distribution don't really matter as long as everyone gets some threshold level of education.

How much control over their children's education are parents entitled to? Few people will answer this question with "none," and few will answer it with "total." Few people think that parents, for example, are entitled to raise their children to despise and be violent toward members of other races, but there is a lot of disagreement about exactly how much control parents are entitled to. For example, may parents use their own advantages to benefit their children educationally? What if parents want to ensure that their children share the parents' values?

What is the public interest in education? Some participants in public debate think the public interest is minimal: the public has an interest in children becoming law-abiding citizens, and that is about it. Others think the public has an interest in children becoming good contributors to public decision-making and to the economy.

How people answer these questions will influence how they approach discussions of educational reform in general and market reform in particular. Those who think the public interest is minimal and parental interest is great will have less reason, prima facie, to oppose markets. But one's stance will also be affected by one's answer to auxiliary questions. Two people might agree, for example, that there is a strong public interest in education, and might even agree exactly what that interest is, but disagree about how well equipped and how well motivated government bureaucrats are as protectors of that interest. How far we trust bureaucrats to choose well, how far we trust parents to choose well, and how far we trust markets to give them good options in the first place are all key variables. Someone who places great weight on parents' interest in raising their children as they see fit has a reason to support the extension of market reform, but such a person may also think that egalitarian distributive outcomes are equally weighty and that markets disrupt those outcomes.

While answers to such questions will influence attitudes toward markets in general, what we finally think about any particular reform must also be informed by our interpretation of the best pertinent evidence that social scientists can produce. In public debates, some enthusiasts of markets and some opponents may sound as if they are immune to evidence. But getting straight on real criteria for supporting or opposing some reform or set of reforms enables us to make better use of the evidence. We will want evidence about how particular reforms will affect the realization of the values we think we have reason to care about, and if we are intellectually honest, we will make our final judgments about specific reforms based on the evidence about that, not on our general ideological preferences for or against markets.

In what follows we debate markets in education in these terms, focusing heavily but not exclusively on the US education system and on the education of children (those under age eighteen). Each of us hopes to persuade the reader that his point of view is right. But our greater ambition is to provide a resource that helps readers to understand the philosophical and institutional issues, see how they relate, and decide for themselves.

NOTE

1. Harry Brighouse and Kailey Mullane, "Aims and Purposes of a State Schooling System: The Case of California," in *Getting Down to Facts 2*, ed. Susanna Loeb (Stanford, CA: Policy Analysis for California Education, 2018).

PART I

HUMAN CAPITAL IN THE TWENTY-FIRST CENTURY

DAVID SCHMIDTZ

WHAT ARE MARKETS?

In a marketplace, people show up offering goods and services. If all goes well, there is an offer, then there is uptake, and a deal has been made. Presupposed by ideas of offer and uptake—of buying and selling—is that people have a right to say no and walk away from the market with whatever they initially brought. Services transfer only if both buyer and seller consent.

When people relate only by consent, they are treating each other as self-owners, that is, as beings with a right to say no. Respecting persons—treating them *as persons*—starts with respecting their right to say no.

In a marketplace, sellers show up, aspiring to be of service, when showing up is safe—that is, when they expect their right to say no to be respected. In a realistically typical transaction between informed adults, anything and everything can go wrong, but usually the dealmaking works out pretty well. Normally when we venture into marketplaces as we experience them in the real world, we find what we are looking for at a price we are willing to pay. We go home without major regret about having bought or sold. Sometimes we fail to find what we are looking for and come home empty-handed. Or, worse, we make a deal but discover that the product is not what we thought, and we wish we had not bought it after all.

Sometimes what hurts the most is discovering that we could have gotten a better deal. Oddly, that particular disappointment consists not in finding that the marketplace had less to offer than we expected but in finding that it had more. We resolve to do better next time, not because the product was not everything we were expecting for the price but because we now realize that the market was offering something even better.

In markets at their observable best, the right to say no is bilateral. Buyers and sellers alike have a right to walk away if what they are offered is not good enough. This right to say no has a crucial two-sided effect—namely, it *enables* buyers to look for something better to buy even as it *motivates* sellers to look for something better to sell.

Whatever is good about market society at its observable, realistic best boils down to this bilateral right to say no. Whatever is good about market society boils down to how well it works as a way of institutionalizing an expectation that people will respect each other as self-owners.

In Western market societies today, we see progress wherever we look. Or maybe not everywhere. When we look at our schools, we see them limping along, muddling through, perhaps not doing crippling damage but not inspiring students, either. I think it would be a mistake to casually treat the current state of education as a crisis. We talk in provocative ways to make ourselves feel important, but when we speak of crisis, we invite panic, and panic confuses, making it seem rational to grasp at straws. The truth is that gradual progress adds up. Gradual progress is not to be confused with failure.[1]

It is rudimentary realism to say our schools are not all they could be. But finding out how good a school can be involves letting schools make gradual progress, and learning from experience what is possible. In the real world, we learn from experience which visions are bad, including which once-great ideas have become obsolete.

Creative Destruction

Blockbuster Video was a spectacularly successful business for a time. Now Blockbuster is gone and no one misses it. The gale of creative destruction that is the marketplace found a better use for resources otherwise wasted on a service whose time had passed. Markets let customers sort out the relative merits of services offered by Netflix versus Blockbuster, and sort they did.

No one appointed a commission to judge whether Blockbuster was too big to fail. In Blockbuster's case, no one was persuaded that we owe it to inferior providers to insulate them from the tide of progress. Nevertheless, in a real marketplace, we can anticipate that entrenched providers will come to have mixed feelings about competition. (How did Blockbuster feel about being crushed by Netflix? Perhaps it went down celebrating cutthroat capitalism. Probably not.) Often, formerly innovative providers get comfortable with established market share, come to see innovation as a threat, then hire lobbyists. We may sympathize, but when businesses shift from being of service to customers to being of service to politicians—buying and selling political power to insulate themselves from the imperative to serve customers—there are consequences.

This is the other end of the realistic spectrum, markets at their observable worst, when companies are heavily subsidized and products become expensive and obsolete. This indefensible variation on the theme of market logic operates in many industries, including publicly funded and publicly delivered systems of education.

Neither Harry Brighouse nor I am simply for or against markets per se. We agree that many things should be for sale, but not all. Real issues concern the marketing of particular services in a given time and place. What happens, Harry and I sometimes worry, when we let *those* people buy and sell *that* service, even as we respect their right to walk away if unsatisfied?

Both of us want our schools to be as good as schools can be. So we won't debate whether to be subject to the tides of supply and demand, because the point is moot. Being subject to those tides is like being subject to gravity. The real question is when and how fighting tides of consumer demand might be worth the cost.

How do producers ever know whether a product is worth its cost?

If you are making electrical wiring for customers you will never meet, and you need to decide whether to use copper or platinum, how do you decide? You do not need markets to tell you not to use aluminum, because aluminum does not work as a conductor of electricity. But you do need markets to tell you whether copper works better than platinum given the opportunity cost of diverting resources (including precious metals) from other purposes.

If customers complain that aluminum wire does not have the conductivity properties they look for in electrical wire, you cannot just say, "That isn't a market decision. It's too important." You have to let markets tell you when to stop trying to force your product on customers who do not want what does not work. Or what fails to do the job cost-effectively.

What Are Markets in Education?

There are markets in education (1) insofar as students or students' parents have a choice about who will teach them; (2) insofar as administrators of schools have a choice about who will teach their clients; (3) insofar as sellers of educational services choose what to charge for their product and buyers choose whether to pay. I guardedly favor markets in education in these three senses. I say "guardedly" because rising quality of service ultimately will depend on how well any system resists decaying into cronyism. Above all, however, consumers should almost always be free to walk away from sellers of inferior products. Consumers have to be free to decline to let you spend their money on aluminum wire.

Is there a special problem with markets in education? Maybe. Markets give customers incentive and opportunity to grow up fast and be as autonomous as they can be. The right to say no and walk away from inferior providers is the core logic of markets. To be worth defending, that right cannot be a mere formality but must instead be a set of robustly affordable options on the ground. That implies a fighting chance of gathering solid information about the costs and benefits of deciding one way rather than another.

Moreover, there is a point before which treating students as autonomous customers would be premature. Markets in child education engage clients whose autonomy is very much in doubt. In general, we are more or less comfortable with a principle of "buyer beware," but not when clients are young children. So how should we market a product that involves teaching the skills to be a market participant in the first place? Someone has to represent young children and take responsibility for walking away from a provider whose service is not good enough. Who can be trusted to know enough and care enough to represent a child effectively? Is anyone guaranteed to care?

There is no guarantee that students, or even parents, will care as much as they should. So, given the lack of guarantees, should we go over parents' heads and give someone else the power to decide? Why? Are contests for power within a bureaucracy *guaranteed* to be won by someone who cares more about a child than the child's own parents?

If I were asking for guarantees, I'd ask for that one first.

The Emergence of the Smart Shopper

Purchasers of automobiles are no longer helpless. They do their research online. Consumers of healthcare services likewise are more sophisticated than they were a generation ago. Within a day of receiving a disturbing diagnosis, patients know much of what medical specialists know about treatment options or about whether they need a second opinion. Similarly, the idea that increasingly well-informed parents should defer to experts becomes less plausible by the day. Everyone's judgment is questionable some of the time. But parents care about getting their facts right.

Moreover, here is one further fact: parents learn not only, nor even mainly, from their own experience. When it is time to gather information, people are not hermits choosing in a vacuum. Parents observe, consult neighbors, and learn fast. Information about particular teachers and schools may not reach Washington, but local communities know, if anyone does.

Where do we see creative people pouring their hearts into bringing better alternatives to market? Why don't we see it everywhere? If, as seems likely, there are no easy answers or magic bullets, then when should we settle for what seems to work tolerably well?

What is the least risky way to test alternatives that might prove to be better?

In general, I would say that when parents are free to learn from mistakes and vote with their feet, providers learn to deliver a superior education.

NOTE

1. See the chapter on freedom of religion in David Schmidtz and Jason Brennan, *A Brief History of Liberty* (Oxford, UK: Wiley-Blackwell, 2010). See also Arthur Herman, *How the Scots Invented the Modern World* (New York: Three Rivers Press, 2001).

1

Charter Schools

THEME: CHARTER SCHOOLS ARE PUBLIC SCHOOLS whose clients have somewhat more opportunity to vote with their feet. Charter schools therefore ought to bring at least some of the discipline and some of the benefits of market provision to our system of education. So, do they?

What falls under the heading of markets in education? We could debate whether the state should get out of education altogether and simply trust consumers and suppliers to find each other. If we did that, we would be trusting consumers to understand and care about the difference between effective and ineffective teachers. We would be trusting providers to have a passion to get better at providing educational services that consumers want. Would such trust be warranted? We have no guarantees, and when it comes to trusting markets, it bothers us that we have no guarantees.

To move in that direction, we would have to cultivate an old-fashioned liberal tolerance for ways in which our neighbors are not like us. What they want for their children need not track what we want for their children. So we have to decide when to say, "It's your life."

VOUCHER SYSTEMS

Less radically, we could try small but potentially significant departures from traditional public schooling. Under a voucher system, the state is left to occupy center stage for all practical purposes, but it aims to give consumers more choice. Using vouchers, parents can put a state-funded public education allowance toward any public or private school. Purists will describe both charter and voucher systems as forms of market socialism. But whatever the terminology, either departure from traditional public education is a small move in the direction of acknowledging twin imperatives to respect consumers and discipline producers in the way that market forces respect consumers and discipline producers.

Everyone should want to know whether that small but possibly significant scope of choice is helping anyone to get a better education. The emerging picture is not decisive.[1] A study by Martin Carnoy for the Economic Policy Institute concludes (and is titled), "School Vouchers Are Not a Proven Strategy for Improving Student Achievement."[2] That conclusion seems fair. If there were any improvement, it would be a consequence of providers responding to the voucher environment by aggressively competing for voucher customers. But why would they? Would they do it for the money? There would have to be a lot of money at stake to tempt a private school to reinvent itself for the sake of recruiting voucher students.

Or perhaps that is asking the wrong question. Perhaps what vouchers mean to private schools is less important than what vouchers mean to public schools. Anya Kamenetz and Cory Turner, of National Public Radio, write:

Where do researchers agree on the impact of choice? Choice programs seem to push nearby public schools to improve. "The results are consistent, and I don't think there's any debate," says Douglas Harris of the Education Research Alliance at Tulane University. "Charters, vouchers and tax credits create competition and positive spillovers." When school choices expand, public schools stand to lose students, and thus money, and they seem to respond by stepping up their game.[3]

Carnegie Mellon economist Dennis Epple notes, "Empirical research on small scale programs does not suggest that awarding students a voucher is a systematically reliable way to improve educational outcomes." On the other hand, "one of the more robust effects" of vouchers is that "competition improves the performance of the public schools that are most closely threatened, for want of a better word, by the voucher program." Ironically, "one of the most consistent benefits of vouchers is enjoyed by students who choose not to use them."[4]

Since 1992 Sweden has operated on a system of vouchers, called *skolpeng*. That system seems to work well enough, but it is not outstanding, and it hardly is obvious that we should emulate it. In a multicultural country such as the United States, we might wonder whether vouchers would do less to help people seeking to educate their children and more to facilitate segregation, even beyond what we already see in America's traditional public schools. Evidence is thin. At this point, it is hard to say.

In the case of charters, there is more data, and trends are becoming apparent. This chapter focuses on charters in part because suggestive data is now emerging. My method is to start with whatever data is available, then look for a theory that fits the data, rather than for data that fits the theory. Making good on that plan is easier said than done, partly because gathering data is hard, partly because it is only human to be more interested in data that fits one's preconceptions. Bias is inescapable, but we can correct for bias to some extent by, for example, having debates. Still, to participate effectively in this forum—to be a partner who is worth the time of someone like Harry—I need to remind myself that I am at a certain career stage: from my perspective, it is too late to care much about winning a debate, but it is never too late to care about learning.

WHAT IS A CHARTER SCHOOL?

Charter schools are hardly an example of a wide-open free market in education. Instead, charters are a small step toward a system of education driven a bit more than are traditional public schools by the mutually adjusting forces of supply and demand. However, although charters are not a big step toward markets in education, neither are they a trivial step.

Like any other public school, charters are publicly funded, and required to meet basic performance standards for public schools. However, charter schools have more autonomy in deciding how to budget and how to meet basic standards. Charters shape their own curricula and tend to have considerable autonomy when it comes to hiring and firing staff. As a general rule, teachers in charter schools are not required to have education degrees. Chemistry teachers in such schools tend to have degrees in chemistry, not education.

Public funding of charter schools is allocated on a per pupil basis, which means that when a student leaves, the public funds that the school was using to educate that student leave along with the student. Thus, whether a school can meet its payroll depends on teachers and administrators attracting and retaining students. In theory, charter schools should aim to do whatever it takes to be places where parents want students to be. If students and parents value learning, then enabling students and parents to express demand for effective learning environments ought to induce providers to invest in meeting that demand. That is the theory, and it would not be the first time that real-world markets had that effect.

So, what are the facts as we know them today? Are charters turning out to be an example of how good markets can be, or of how badly planners fail when they try to marshal cherry-picked virtues of markets? Obviously, I hope charters represent a step forward for American public education, not because I care about charters but because I care about education and would be happy to see any sign of potential for improvement in our system of education in general, including public education. If market forces can help at all in the realm of public education, then charter schools ought to make a detectable difference. So do they?

2009

There is no magic in charter schools. Yet charters may have an advantage over traditional public schools. That advantage over traditional public schools (TPS, as the studies cited here refer to them) does not translate into a guarantee. The anticipated advantage certainly need not translate into immediate results. Indeed, the first well-controlled, well-regarded, and nonpartisan study that I came across, which was carried out by the Center for Research on Education Outcomes (CREDO) in 2009, was inconclusive at best:

> The group portrait shows wide variation in performance. The study reveals that a decent fraction of charter schools, 17 percent, provide superior education opportunities for their students. Nearly half of the charter schools nationwide have results that are no different from the local public school options and over a third, 37 percent, deliver learning results that are significantly worse than their students would have realized had they remained in traditional public schools.[5]

That is not what I expected, and it was sobering. My first reaction: TPS are not performing at the level we want. So for 37 percent of charters to perform *below* that level is discouraging. The CREDO study was the best available at the time, and it told us that, to be blunt, charter schools are not what we are looking for.

One glimmer of hope: there might be a gale of creative destruction, a harsh market discipline that would liquidate the underperforming 37 percent, yet which would leave standing the high-performing 17 percent. After all, that gale of creative destruction, as Joseph Schumpeter taught us, is essentially what market forces amount to.

Or is it? What else would market forces be?

2013

The information on charter schools that began to come out in 2009 did not come close to suggesting that charters were solving problems with traditional public schooling. Was I wrong to see competitive market forces at work in the field of charter public education? If charters do marshal forces of market competition, why isn't competition working in education as it works in other industries?

Will competition shake out a better long-run result? Perhaps the 17 percent of charters that were outperforming TPS in 2009 would survive the discipline of consumer choice. The survival of high-performing charters would, on its face, be a good thing no matter what else was happening. Moreover, high-performing schools would operate according to business models that at least some future charters, and perhaps some TPS, could and would emulate. (If the TPS were raising their game to another level by emulating the innovations of charter schools, then comparing charters with a rising TPS baseline would mask absolute progress, but that would be a welcome result regardless of whether it compromised our data.) Models of success might become a larger percentage of the population of schools going forward.

When I visited Stanford in 2008 to gather my first thoughts on the ethics and economics of education, I learned about the research that Eric Hanushek and his colleagues at Stanford were conducting at the time. I admit that when I looked at the materials they were compiling for that first report, the tangible advantages of charter schools seemed, let's say, not so tangible.

To me, it was common sense that charter schools are a better type of public school—even if only slightly better— but I stopped expecting the data ever to confirm that charters were *significantly* better. So I was as surprised as anyone when later studies began to paint a different picture. Here is the CREDO study's 2013 update:

> We found 25 percent of charter schools had significantly stronger growth than their TPS counterparts in reading, 56 percent were not significantly different and 19 percent of charter schools had weaker growth. In math, the results show that 29 percent of charter schools had stronger growth than their TPS counterparts, 40 percent had growth that was not significantly different, and 31 percent had weaker growth. These results are an improvement over those in the 2009 report.[6] (2013, 56).

This sounds like a modest improvement. However, another trend was becoming apparent:

> Learning gains improve significantly for charter students by their second year of enrollment—seeing about 22 more days of learning in reading and 14 more days in math. Once a student is enrolled for four or more years, their learning gains outpace TPS by 50 days in reading and 43 days in math per year.[7]
> On average, students attending charter schools have eight additional days of learning in reading and the same days of learning in math per year compared to their peers in traditional public schools . . . with the relative performance of the charter sector improving each year.[8]

The emerging trend seemed to be that new schools in 2013 were just as hit-or-miss as new schools had been in 2009, but established charters had learned something.

> Looking at just the *continuing* schools in 2013, students at these same charter schools had about seven more days of

learning than their TPS counterparts in reading. Results for charter students in *new* schools mirror the 2009 findings: students at new schools have significantly lower learning gains in reading than their TPS peers.[9]

The somewhat pessimistic interpretation of this is that charter schools are not inherently better except in the sense that they are, after all, subject to the Darwinian logic of creative destruction in the same way that Blockbuster Video was. That is, the worst schools are the ones most likely to disappear, which by itself accounts for a gradual relative improvement over TPS and a rising average level of measurable relative performance. If the process were merely Darwinian and nothing more, and thus if the appearance of new "mutations" in the population were a random process, then there would be two ways to look at it. On the upside, there would be a driving dynamic of rising average charter performance, simply because high-performing schools would last longer than underperformers and would be a more enduring part of the statistical pool. On the downside, because of the essential randomness of new mutations, we would always expect new schools to be all over the map performance-wise.

However, there is more to the marketplace than creative destruction. In addition to the remorseless Darwinian logic created by buyers voting with their feet—declining to do repeat business with sellers who underperform—there is a further fact: in a market ecosystem, what is selected, and thus what survives, is the ideas of sellers, not their literal genomes. A seller's idea is not a random mutation passively selected over generations; rather, sellers learn as they go how to be selected. Seventeen percent of charters were learning to be what buyers are selecting. Not only are those higher-performing charters more likely to be found, more likely to be selected, and more likely to survive, but they are also more likely to be emulated. Genes can't be emulated, but ideas can.

Meanwhile, students in underperforming schools get hurt. Or, less depressingly but more accurately, students in underperforming schools are not helped as much as they would have been helped by a better education. That will remain the case even as parents differentially give up on underperforming schools, and thus even as underperforming schools ultimately close, thereby driving progress in average charter performance as measured by aggregate statistics.

Is there an increasing tendency for start-up schools to be quicker learners, better able to draw upon a growing body of successful experience? Available data weighs against being too optimistic:

> The new charter schools in the original 16 states that recently opened or had students mature into tested grades appear to look a lot like the 2009 results in average student growth. Their performance is worse than that of the continuing charters. But other factors play out as well: low-performing schools are not being shut quickly enough and some low-performing schools are being permitted to replicate. When the total stock of charter schools (continuing and new) is considered, there is slight improvement relative to the TPS alternative but no absolute gains in learning.[10]

Note the phrase "permitted to replicate." What does it mean for charters to be "permitted to replicate"? What does it mean for charters to not be shut down quickly enough? I had been operating under the assumption that what shuts down a charter is parents taking their children elsewhere. Did I misunderstand? Reading between the lines, I had to suspect that even in the charter sector, decisions to shut schools are made from the top down rather than from the bottom up. Is it true? Do charter schools shut down only when legislatures or school boards revoke their charters?

First, to be clear, I never question the need for regulatory oversight. For example, the plausible assumption that the world's great restaurants are all private is consistent with the plausible assumption that restaurants need to be regulated by public health and safety inspectors. We may likewise suppose that parents are presumptively the best caretakers of their children without denying that child protective services need to be on the lookout for abusive parents. We don't need to oversimplify such realities to acknowledge the value to society of market competition. Accordingly, in the same way that the restaurant industry can be well served by independent health and safety inspectors, we may want boards to monitor all public schools, including charters, to certify that they are providing the kind of service we expect.

Yet my curiosity remains. What is the primary discipline here? Is it the threat of school boards revoking a charter, or the threat of parents leaving and thereby cutting a school's budget? It is a relevant factual question, and I have only limited information. Some indication of what closes a charter school comes from the Center for Education Reform, which (for example) lists 174 charter school closings in Arizona between 1996 and 2011. The list is not, of course, a controlled scientific experiment, but scanning reasons mentioned for the school closings is suggestive. Of the 174, four were closed by the district, according to the report. Another eighteen are listed as closed due to poor academic performance. Forty-two are listed as closed due to mismanagement: failure to comply with charter laws, inadequate or false record-keeping, and misappropriation of state funds. Assuming that these three categories are all initiated at the district level and adding the three numbers yields a rough guess; I put no stock in the precision of these numbers, but they imply that nearly half of the closings in Arizona between 1996 and 2011—64 of 174 school closings—may have been mandated from above by district monitors.

On the other side, 84 of 174 closings were for financial reasons, the most often specified of which was inadequate enrollment. The remaining two dozen or so closings were for "other" reasons, including inadequate facilities and changing life circumstances of school operators (illness, retirement, and so on). Thus it appears that nearly half (perhaps more) of the closings were initiated by schools themselves, as clients said no to what they were trying to sell.[11] Was the regulatory oversight harder on charters than on TPS? I do not know. Neither do I have any opinion on whether it should be.[12]

It is crucial here to remind ourselves that charter schools are not a revolutionary alternative to traditional public schools. Rather, they are a variation on the general model of public school. Let's not exaggerate the difference. The difference is not that charters are not subject to public administration, but that in limited ways charters are subject not only to public oversight but also to the forces of consumer demand. Thus, we can hope that an underperforming charter can underperform only for a while: only for however long it takes a school to acquire a reputation for underperformance and for parents to get wise and abandon ship. By contrast, high-performing schools make for a better-educated population so long as they continue to outperform. By itself, that should make for a gradually rising overall performance level.

Here are some further caveats. We still need a clearer picture of how charter school performance is affected by demographics. Perhaps there is some systematic, identifiable difference that predicts which charter schools will outperform TPS and which will languish. For example, the authors of a Massachusetts study note in passing a typical feature of the more subscribed charters in their study: most of them had a "no excuses" policy (which is to say, high standards both behaviorally and academically, more time spent on academics, and a focus on building culture and community values).[13] Perhaps that kind of environment is what all students need, and what many TPS fail to provide. I do not know.

Or perhaps we can predict that charters work better for some populations than for others, and plan accordingly. For example, does it matter whether a population of children is urban or rural? Does it matter whether the students are white or black, male or female? Does it matter whether a charter school has a religious orientation? If so, how exactly does it matter? Are there charter schools that, upon close inspection, are not genuinely offering open enrollment in the way that public schools are legally required to do? If so, what should we infer?

EVALUATING CHARTERS

A Rand Corporation study concludes:

> Students who attended charter high schools were more likely to graduate and go on to college. For the locations for which charter–high school graduation and college attendance rates were available—Chicago and Florida—the researchers found that attending a charter high school appeared to boost a student's probability of graduating by 7 to 15 percentage points. Similarly, students who attended a charter high school appeared to benefit from an 8 to 10 percentage point increase in the likelihood that they would enroll in college. Although there are some limitations to these results, they provide reason for encouragement in terms of the long-term benefits of charter schools. They also suggest a need to look beyond test scores to fully assess charter schools' performance.[14]

Whether charters are succeeding is substantially a factual question, but measurement is a problem. Chapter 2 focuses on measurement problems. Here, suffice it to say that problems with measuring the performance of charters cannot be ignored. Charters offer "open enrollment," which means they operate by the same admission standards as any other public school. When there are more applicants than seats in the school, seats are allocated by random lottery. Or are they? "Cream-skimming" (selecting students more likely to excel on the standardized tests to which all public school students are subjected) violates regulations. However, if cream-skimming is the easy way to create an appearance of a successful learning environment, then we should not be surprised to see implicit cream-skimming in retention decisions even if cream-skimming does not factor into admission decisions. It is no mistake to wonder about the costs and benefits of that. What happens when we take the best students out of the TPS? What becomes of them? What becomes of students left behind? Further, does cream-skimming skew the measuring? Again, this is a factual question. But the concern is that what shows up as statistical evidence of a more successful learning environment might simply be more selective retention. So, what do we know?

> Due to the use of matched pairs of charter and TPS students in this analysis, this study cannot address whether charter schools manipulate their recruitment to obtain more academically prepared students, known as cream-skimming. Such a test would require us to retrace the steps of students transferring into charter schools back to their prior feeder school and anchor their academic performance there among the students from their former school. These topics deserve further study. What we can say, however, is that the demographic trends since the earlier report point to more challenging students, not less, which would run counter to the notion of selectivity on prior education performance. CREDO also found suggestive evidence that students had falling scores in TPS in the two years prior to their switch to charter schools, which also runs counter to the cream skimming hypothesis.[15]

Everyone robustly and predictably responds to incentives, including perverse incentives. I have made a career out of studying incentive structures and what we should be learning from them about moral and political ideals, so

I am the last person to want to sweep problems of perverse incentives under the rug. The true virtue of markets is not that there can never be perverse incentives in a real marketplace or that providers would never respond to perverse incentives. The true virtue of markets at their realistic best is that they empower consumers to *protect* themselves from perverse incentives. How? By empowering consumers to walk away from providers whose product is inferior.

Markets do only so much, and guarantee even less. People who exaggerate their need for guarantees are driven to pretend that where there are no *guaranteed* benefits, there are no benefits, period. But we live in a world of observable correlation, not a world of guarantees.

I have not explored the case for private as opposed to public funding, or for privately as opposed to publicly run schools. The point of this chapter is to examine public schools at their realistic best, where public schools at their realistic best may turn out to be the emerging institution of charter schools.

In any case, barring a clinching argument, we should suspect that it is better not to be overconfident, and instead to leave parents free to thoroughly test all available alternatives. Admittedly, if parents are experimenting with other people's money, that is, with tax money, that implies a responsibility to impose some limits on a parent's right to keep spending money on schools that are proven failures. Still, this bit of common sense remains: if we aim to limit people's propensity to spend money on proven failures, parents are not the ones who pose the greatest risk. The greater risk comes from decision-makers who would use other people's money to foist defective products on customers. Knowing that customers would walk away from defective products if they could, corrupt decision-makers respond not by making sure their product is not defective but by making sure customers have no right to walk away.

POVERTY

We are learning about charter schools. Both the general logic of the incentive structures and the first generation of performance measures seem slowly to be pointing in favor of charters as a vehicle for delivering public education. As of 2013, the CREDO study concluded, "the charter school sector has improved in most states since the 2009 report."[16]

Perhaps most encouraging is the apparent impact on minorities. "Black students who attend a charter school on average have 14 additional days of learning in both reading and math compared to black students enrolled in TPS," the report notes. Breaking this down further, "black students in poverty who attend charter schools gain an additional 29 days of learning in reading and 36 days in math per year over their TPS counterparts." And "the biggest impacts are among Hispanic students who are English language learners; they gain 50 additional days of learning in reading and 43 additional days in math from charter attendance per year."[17]

> Charter schools and their feeder schools are educating more disadvantaged students than in 2009. Across the 27 states in this study, more than half of the charter students live in poverty. . . . These shifts reflect growth in the proportion of disadvantaged parents that is aware, is informed and is comfortable exercising their options for school choice. The typical

charter student arrives at a charter school with lower levels of educational performance than was the case in 2009.[18]

Initially I vaguely pictured charter schools as roughly like an upper-class British prep school, but events are proving me increasingly wrong as years go by. Some private schools were and are like that, but charter schools are evolving into something distinct. They increasingly are serving children whose parents want something unlike TPS they have known, while still wanting what in their eyes is good about public schools. They just want more choice.

POVERTY 2015

Yet another update of the CREDO study came out in 2015:

1. Our findings show urban charter schools in the aggregate provide significantly higher levels of annual growth in both math and reading compared to their TPS peers.
2. Learning gains for charter school students are larger by significant amounts for Black, Hispanic, low-income, and special education students in both math and reading.[19]

For example:

In each region, the percent of students in poverty or who were Black or Hispanic was positively associated with learning gains in both math and reading across the regions. While the results might be counter-intuitive—these groups are typically considered less academically prepared—the correlations are consistent with the expressed mission of many urban charter school operators to provide high-quality education choices specifically for these students.[20]

This is important for at least two reasons. First, these urban regions can serve as models from which all public schools serving disadvantaged student populations may learn. Second, and perhaps more important, these charter sectors clearly refute the idea that some groups of students cannot achieve high levels of academic success. They need only to be given the opportunity.[21]

At the same time,

despite the overall positive learning impacts, there are urban communities in which the majority of the charter schools lag the learning gains of their TPS counterparts, some to distressingly large degrees. In some urban areas, cities have no schools that post better gains than their TPS alternatives and more than half the schools are significantly worse.[22]

I am not confident of my (or anyone's) ability to sort out what all of this means. It may mean that students try out a charter school to learn whether it is right for them. Students for whom a school is not working keep looking for another option. Students who stay for a second year are the ones who thrive in that setting. If that is the case, that is not so much a vindication of charter schools per se as of students and parents simply having opportunities.

I also infer that if we look at our best TPS, and if they tend to be white suburban schools, we should not be surprised to find that charters with similar demographics get similar results. Suburban charters may attract better than average teachers, but so do suburban TPS, and suburban TPS are the statistical baselines for charters with suburban demographics. Again, I could be wrong. There are untold numbers of uncontrolled variables operating here. One bottom line: where there is no problem with TPS, charter schools do not solve a problem. However, if black, Hispanic, and inner city populations are better served by charter schools than by TPS, then charters give us a real alternative precisely where we desperately need real alternatives.[23]

I wish I could end this chapter with three cheers for charters, confident in our public system's willingness and ability to reinvent itself as an institution that swims with rather than against the tide of market forces. What I am seeing is more interesting and more inconclusive than that. A Massachusetts study reports an impressive closing of the gap between the test scores of black and white students in Boston charters.[24] The study was based on charters that were oversubscribed and thus had to allocate seats by lottery: a natural experiment comparing students accepted by lottery versus students rejected. On the other hand, although the study could take advantage of a natural experimental control when it came to evaluating students, it seems highly likely that the charters themselves were not a random sample. After all, they were the schools that assigned seats by lottery, which means that they were the schools for which demand for seats exceeded supply, which means that they were the schools in greatest demand by parents and students. Should we predict that those schools were outliers rather than typical charters? I would. I began this chapter by acknowledging that to have faith in consumer demand in the arena of education is to trust parents and students to understand and care about the difference between effective and ineffective schooling. If we suppose that parents and children can be trusted to demand excellent education, then the Boston charters in this study, being the most in demand, presumably also were not only better than TPS but better than other charters for which there was less demand.

That leaves us with some uncertainty about the generality of this exceedingly hopeful result. Unfortunately, segregation undoubtedly is a serious problem in TPS. Are charters any better? It is easy to imagine that giving families more choice could lead them to avoid schools where they would be in a minority. That may be all it takes to drive spontaneous demographic shifts that in practice amount to segregation—voluntary, yes, but still generally unintended and unwanted. On the other hand, it seems that such documented successes as we currently are seeing are turning out to be concentrated among urban minorities. That gives us some reason to be, at a minimum, willing to let the experiment continue. That is all a proponent of markets asks for, anyway.

One general caution here is that our reasons to make peace with creative destruction—with holding providers accountable for the excellence of their product—could be translated as reasons to abandon change-resisting unionization. One benefit of declining unionization is declining labor costs, and perhaps an increase in the extent to which teachers on the ground hold themselves, and are held, individually accountable. I understand why socialists would resist this, although I think they are wrong. And yet the rest of us also need to be clear that the reason to resist unionization is to preserve individual accountability, not to deprive workers of bargaining power. If the wages of non-unionized professional teachers do not rise soon, unions will come back. Someone needs to invent administrative structures (teacher cooperatives, perhaps?) that enable parents and students to invest directly neither in union bosses nor in upper-level administration but in teachers who deliver.[25]

None of this is an argument against government provision; neither is it an argument against government funding. But it is an argument against No Child Left Behind (2001 legislation imposing federal education standards across the United States) or any totalizing, colonizing, centralizing impulse—big business or big government—on the provider side. Consumers need to find out what does not work. It is customers, the ostensible beneficiaries, who are best equipped to know and care whether the benefits they are supposedly receiving are real. When consumers are not free to walk away, providers keep providing what does not work. Choice disciplines providers. It has never been a panacea, but neither has humanity ever had a better alternative.

As chains of charter schools emerge, succeed, and proliferate, I expect some of them to become victims of their own success, insofar as they take a successful model and try to scale it up. Scale is part of the essence of an organizational structure. That is to say, a scaled-up organization is not merely a replica of a small one. It is a different structure and it will operate by a different logic. As organizations grow, the top level gets further from the ground where the feedback is. The upper echelon of a school's administration increasingly comes to be interacting more with accountants than with students. Schools may not develop the runaway pathologies of government agencies that get too big, but they will develop the pathologies of corporations that get too big. So long as a given school is not the only game in town, though, customers will come, and eventually go, more or less as Blockbuster Video's customers came and went.

No one should imagine that as we see the success stories emerge, we can simply scale them up. Success is not that simple. Markets react to the success stories in the right way. No one attempts to bureaucratize them and operate them on a national scale. Rather, market agents learn from them, and any market-driven scaling is driven one franchise at a time, with locally situated and personally accountable agents learning as they go, and getting shut down if they don't learn fast. The thing is, sometimes it works. Not always, but sometimes.

This note of cautious optimism might be most apt in the case of charter schools that outperform TPS serving comparably disadvantaged demographics. It depends on why those charters seem to be outperforming TPS in serving the disadvantaged. Perhaps TPS faculty in the poorest neighborhoods consist largely of teachers who would rather be elsewhere but who cannot compete for better jobs, whereas charter faculty in the poorest neighborhoods consist largely of teachers who are in those neighborhoods because that is where their heart is. Is that why charters outperform TPS in the poorest schools? I do not know. It might be. If it is, then that is a difference that top-down bureaucrats cannot simply scale up. What can bureaucrats do? Perhaps the best they can do is stay out of the way and let high-performing charters evolve as beacons that signal how inspiring the life of a teacher can be.

Another way in which charters could become victims of their own success is this: as idealistic and mission-driven founders of charter schools succeed, and as head-turning amounts of money begin to gush in, there may come a point when the reputations of particular charters are so solid that a charter can make even more money by hiring less-expensive teachers. Quality of instruction need not decrease immediately, since young teachers straight out of college might be happy to start at low salaries in order to be part of such an inspiring mission. The quality of teachers might drop off only very slowly. It would happen as these young teachers enter their prime earning years. They come to expect substantial raises commensurate with the professional excellence they have achieved, only to find themselves being laid off instead, replaced by cheap new graduates in their early twenties. That is when the special "no excuses" esprit de corps of a formerly high-performing charter will crash, not before.

COLLEGE VERSUS K–12

I have been talking about K–12. Where students are adults, they need not be patronized. They can decide for themselves whether a college is what they are looking for. It makes sense to have private colleges. It also makes sense to have programs offering financial assistance to students who would not otherwise be able to afford the expense of college. Financial assistance could come from private or public sources. Public funding does not imply public provision.

What is different about college is how rapidly the underlying business model is changing. Colleges are not what colleges were even ten years ago, and are not what colleges will be ten years from now. Academic departments likely will become increasingly accountable for covering their own payrolls and even for the cost of leasing their space.

Departments will cover costs with tuition revenues, research grants, and private gifts. Deans and department heads realize how far this process has already gone; rank-and-file faculty often remain unaware.

Tenured faculty are basically a financial bubble, emerging only a few generations ago and not sustainable indefinitely. Faculty who now picture themselves as independent scholars increasingly will be reminded that they are salespeople. Faculty already understand the imperative to sell their product to students and to readers. Debating whether to be subject to that tide is moot. The live question is how to cope. I have no especially encouraging answer. My only conjecture is the obvious one: namely, that universities increasingly will be run by people who understand, accept, and creatively respond to the upheaval already under way.

One notorious aspect of a school's certification mission is the problem of grade inflation. Theoretically, the market should pay a premium for schools that can establish a reputation for providing an honest signal. We know from observation, however, that whatever pressure there is to provide an honest signal, it is not enough, and grade inflation is ubiquitous.

Some think the problem is like this: Schools are eager to sell whatever pretense customers are willing to buy, lest customers begin shopping for graders with a reputation for being even more indiscriminate. However, if students can find out whether a given grader is indiscriminate, then anyone can find out. In the limit, this essentially does away with grading altogether. A faux certification, understood to be no signal at all of true education, would be a certification for which there were no customers. The real problem is something else.

The harder truth: The exercise of grading could be a crucially important pedagogical tool if only teachers had the time, but they don't. Colleges are in no position to give faculty credit for spending their time that way. The real problem is not pressure from student-customers so much as time pressure. Conscientious grading does not pay. That is the culprit. Faculty give the highest grades they can give without shame, thereby minimizing time spent dealing with students who want advice on how to improve. Law schools seem to have some success in marketing reputations for having strict grading curves, but I have no information on how well curving grades translates into learning outcomes.

NOTES

1. Dennis Epple, Richard E. Romano, and Miguel Urquiola, "School Vouchers: A Survey of the Economics Literature," *Journal of Economic Literature* 55, no. 2 (2017): 441–492. See also R. J. Waddington and M. Berends, "Early Impacts of the Indiana Choice Scholarship Program: Achievement Effects for Students in Upper Elementary and Middle School," paper presented at the Society for Research on Educational Effectiveness Spring 2017 Conference, Washington, DC, revised version. See also Jonathan N. Mills and Patrick J. Wolf, "How Has the Louisiana Scholarship Program Affected Students? A Comprehensive Summary of Effects After Three Years," Education Research Alliance for New Orleans, June 26, 2017, https://educationresearchalliancenola.org/files/publications/ERA1706-Policy-Brief-Louisiana-Scholarship-Program_170804_161627.pdf.
2. Martin Carnoy, "School Vouchers Are Not a Proven Strategy for Improving Student Achievement," Economic Policy Institute, Washington, DC, February 28, 2017, http://www.epi.org/files/pdf/121635.pdf.

3. Anya Kamenetz and Cory Turner, "Why It's So Hard to Know Whether School Choice Is Working," National Public Radio, May 21, 2017, https://www.npr.org/sections/ed/2017/05/21/522051355/why-its-so-hard-to-know-whether-school-choice-is-working.

4. Cory Turner, Eric Weddle, and Peter Balonon-Rosen, "The Promise and Peril of School Vouchers," National Public Radio, May 12, 2017, http://www.npr.org/sections/ed/2017/05/12/520111511/the-promise-and-peril-of-school-vouchers.

5. CREDO, *Multiple Choice: Charter School Performance in 16 States* (Stanford, CA: Center for Research on Education Outcomes, 2009), 1.

6. CREDO, *National Charter School Study 2013* (Stanford, CA: Center for Research on Education Outcomes, 2013), 56.

7. CREDO, *National Charter School Study 2013*, 79.

8. CREDO, *National Charter School Study 2013*, 3.

9. CREDO, *National Charter School Study 2013*, 29, emphasis added.

10. CREDO, *National Charter School Study 2013*, 83.

11. Alison Consoletti, "The State of Charter Schools: What We Know—and What We Do Not Know—About Performance and Accountability," Center for Education Reform, Washington, DC, December 2011, Appendix D, "Closed Charter Schools by State: National Data 2011," https://www.edreform.com/wp-content/uploads/2011/12/CER_FINALClosedSchools2011-1.pdf.

12. For what it is worth, a Massachusetts study suggests that charters indeed appear to face more stringent accountability requirements than do traditional public schools. The state Charter School Office reviews and makes recommendations on charter applications, reviews the performance of existing charter schools, and decides whether charters should be renewed. Charter schools are held accountable via annual reports, financial audits, and site visits, and are required to file for renewal every five years. Renewal applications must show that a school's academic program is successful, that the school is a viable organization, and that it has been faithful

to its charter. Since 1994, the state has received a total of 350 charter applications and has granted 76. Eight of the 76 Massachusetts charters were surrendered or revoked as of fall 2009. Atila Abdulkadiroglu, Joshua D. Angrist, Susan M. Dynarski, Thomas J. Kane, and Parag A. Pathak, "Accountability and Flexibility in Public Schools: Evidence from Boston's Charters and Pilots," *Quarterly Journal of Economics* 126 (2011): 705.

13. Max Bean, "The No-Excuses Charter School Movement," *Dewey to Delpit* (blog), http://edcommentary.blogspot.co.uk/ p/no-excuses-charter-movement.html.

14. Ron Zimmer, Brian Gill, Kevin Booker, Stephane Lavertu, Tim R. Sass, and John Witte, "Are Charter Schools Making a Difference? A Study of Student Outcomes in Eight States," RAND Corporation Research Brief, 2009, 2, https:// www.rand.org/pubs/research_briefs/RB9433.html.

15. CREDO, *National Charter School Study 2013*, 82.

16. CREDO, *National Charter School Study 2013*, 43.

17. CREDO, *National Charter School Study 2013*, 65, 81.

18. CREDO, *National Charter School Study 2013*, 82.

19. CREDO, *Urban Charter School Study: Report on 41 Regions 2015* (Stanford, CA: Center for Research on Education Outcomes, 2015), v.

20. CREDO, *Urban Charter School Study 2015*, 36.

21. CREDO, *Urban Charter School Study 2015*, 38.

22. CREDO, *Urban Charter School Study 2015*, vi.

23. On this note, one of the perversities of measurement could turn out in this case to be a blessing. If schools are chartered with a mission of catering to the most disadvantaged populations, then the statistical comparison class for these schools would be the TPS with the same demographics—that is, those TPS that likewise cater disproportionately to the most disadvantaged students. In that case, charters could contrive to put themselves in a position to advertise what would be, after all, a virtue that is as genuine as it is measurable: namely, documented high performance in serving the most disadvantaged students.

24. Among students attending regular public middle schools, blacks score about 0.7σ below whites in language arts and 0.8σ below whites in math. The charter school effects reported here are therefore large enough to reduce the black-white reading gap in middle school by two-thirds. The even larger estimated gains in math (about 0.4σ) are more than enough to eliminate the racial gap in math while students are in middle school. Effects of roughly 0.2σ estimated for high school ELA and math are large enough to close the black-white high school gap of about 0.8σ in both subjects assuming four years of charter high school enrollment (Abdulkadiroglu et al., "Accountability and Flexibility in Public Schools," 746).

25. In passing, I note one other variation on the theme of attempting to reinvent public schools so as to make sellers of educational services more responsive to consumers. In the United Kingdom, "academisation" involves converting a failing traditional public school into an academy— something resembling what Americans would call a charter school. Where a charter is a new institution, an academy is a new institution that displaces an old one. It stands to reason that among displaced faculty and staff, British academies will be even more controversial and even more disruptive than are American charters. Of course, as noted earlier, incumbent sellers do not favor competition. I am optimistic about how market forces would support British academisation in the long run, but as to whether political forces will support it in the short to medium term, I have no idea. Center for Research on Education Outcomes

2

Be Careful What
You Measure

THEME: IF WE MISREAD OUR EDUCATIONAL mission, we also misread what we (who volunteered for that mission) need to do to be giving people their due. Further, to know whether we are accomplishing our mission, we have to be able to measure, to quantify, but if we pretend there is any straightforward way to do that, we oversimplify.

WHAT IS OUR MISSION?

The mission of teachers (and of schools that employ them) is twofold. Schools hire teachers not only to *educate* students but to *certify* them. In our role as educators, our job is to *develop* talent. As certifiers, our job is to *measure*—to evaluate performance.

The point is not that the missions are unconnected but that making the connection is an achievement. A grade should be an achievement on a student's part, indicating that the student has become educated. Teachers have a responsibility to connect getting good grades to worthwhile learning. Unless we think hard about how to make certification a friend rather than foe of real learning, we are merely going through the motions, and in response, so will most of our students.

For example, we might owe it to our students to avoid using tools of certification that induce cramming. Cramming is, of course, a skill with many uses. If our aim were to teach this skill, then getting students to practice cramming would have value—limited value. Students who cram are working to store undigested material in short-term memory. It is a kind of learning that does not last. It is apt for short-term purposes (such as getting ready for a debate), but it is no substitute for storing information in long-term memory. It has nothing to do with making time for the reflection that goes into developing an independent critical perspective. Therefore, the development of cramming skills is at best a small part of becoming truly educated.

We owe it to our students to ask ourselves: do our certification processes move students toward real learning, or only toward being fleetingly able to deliver a mere appearance?

MAKING IT PAY FOR STUDENTS TO LEARN

One thing a school owes students is to bring its education and certification missions together, and keep them together. Another thing schools owe students is to teach students themselves to take responsibility for bringing those missions together. In other words, schools owe it to students to be places of learning, not places of teaching. Therefore, the twofold mission has to be largely the responsibility of individual students. Students have to learn that a grade is not what they need for success in life. The lesson is not complicated, but students still have to learn it. Moreover, individual students have to learn that their education consists of what they pay attention to. Education is not something going on in the front of the classroom that can be left to the teacher while students tend to their tweeting.

Even some of our best students, needless to say, treat getting educated as a means to the end of getting grades. Teachers, however, must do the opposite. Teachers must treat certification as a means to the end of inducing students to learn. We have a responsibility to our clients as seekers of education that trumps our responsibility to them as seekers of certification. Most clients are wise enough to understand that. Certification is part of the mission, perhaps, but not an ultimate end. To certify is to signal that the person certified has achieved a level of learning, as judged by an institution representing itself as qualified to judge.

It's the Economy

Here is a relevant point about the larger economic context in which schools operate: there is more opportunity and more vertical mobility in some societies than in others. So in my mind, the logic of markets should go like this: Wherever education is enabling people to live better lives, there will be demand for education. Further, wherever there is demand, there will be supply. In other words, wherever returns to excellent education are greatest, that is where we should find the most excellent education. That is where buyers have the most reason to invest in excellence. That is where buyers have the most reason to learn to discern excellence. That is where suppliers have the most reason to respond with excellence.

Where my logic turns out to be wrong, that tells us to look for reasons why. In other words, it tells us that there is something interesting going on. There is a bottleneck somewhere in the system that is preventing that logic from playing itself out in the normal way. A word to the wise here: if we are witnessing deteriorating educational quality, the place to look for an explanation is not necessarily within the institution of education itself. Schools are supposed to serve a larger community along with individual clients. Demand within a community for a higher level of excellence is what gives people opportunities to make a living within that community by meeting that demand. If we want to see rising educational standards, then we should want to let there be increasing returns to rising standards. Raising the returns to being an excellent teacher is important (as discussed in the following section).

However, the real key to progress lies in raising the returns to being an excellent *student*. Where it pays to learn, learning there will be.

Left-wing conservatives (that is, nationalists and populists who think they want to build walls, people who voted for Donald Trump and would have voted for Bernie Sanders) feel oppressed by the fact that lifelong learning is paying increasing rather than decreasing dividends. They want their own level of educational achievement to be the level that pays. They experience progress as a threat. They regard lifelong learning not as the spice of life but as unending and unfair toil with an uncertain payoff. They lament having to be perennially alert to evolving needs and opportunities. They demand shelter from change. They do not see themselves as asserting a right to stop their children from inventing a better world.

MAKING IT PAY FOR TEACHERS TO TEACH

Teachers need to evaluate students. In turn, someone needs to evaluate teachers. These are different tasks, but we have conflated them. As Derek Neal explains:

> Education officials often use one assessment system both to create measures of student achievement and to create performance metrics for educators. However, modern standardized testing systems are not designed to produce performance metrics for teachers or principals. They are designed to produce reliable measures of individual student achievement in a low-stakes testing environment. The design features that promote reliable measurement provide opportunities for teachers to profitably coach students on test-taking skills, and educators typically exploit these opportunities whenever modern assessments are used in high-stakes settings as vehicles for gathering information about their performance. Because these coaching responses often contaminate measures of both student achievement and educator performance, it is likely possible to acquire more accurate measures of both student achievement and education performance by developing separate assessment systems that are designed specifically for each measurement task.[1]

It stands to reason that when we hold teachers accountable, we tend to get a higher level of performance. Still, that is an empirical hypothesis, not an a priori truth. Upon reflection, it is a general truism of economic analysis that if we ask to see result X, and reward teachers enough for showing us result X, then teachers will figure out ways to show us result X.

We have decided, repeatedly, that we need to do better. We need to be responsible. We need to be accountable. Therefore, we need deliverables, which means we need measurables. I understand, and I cannot disagree. Still, we need to be careful what we measure. When we ask for measurables, we tend to get what we ask for—delivered in a sometimes obscenely cost-effective way.[2]

Where there are measures, it is just a matter of time before people begin to play games with those measures.

We do need to measure success in the classroom. But this is so easy to overdo. It is so easy to exaggerate our need for mechanical measures that do not require situated judgment. A better aim might be to enable teachers to generate information that enables teachers who care to make reliable judgments. It is unclear how bureaucrats can help, beyond simply trusting teachers to get the job done plus declining to protect teachers when that trust proves misplaced. In that case, the task is not to certify teachers but to put them in a position where we can trust them.

Accountability movements rise when trust falls and we no longer believe in our teachers. But teachers who believe in themselves hold themselves accountable. The kind of teachers we believe in want to know what works and what does not. If they were free to draw their own conclusions about such information as they can acquire, then instead of being terrorized by data, they would use data to help them understand and shape their own teaching environment. *If they are free to draw their own conclusions, then they will want more information rather than less.*

Thus Jal Mehta notes, "While the United States remains the world leader in assessments and accountability, Finland and Shanghai are leaders in student performance, and they get there in an entirely different way." Mehta recommends treating data not as a disciplinary tool but as information teachers use to understand and shape their teaching environment.[3]

To Mehta, the corrosive reforms are the ones that simply put more pressure on teachers.[4] When we use student test scores to evaluate teachers, then the *teachers* are the ones being tested. When we do that, teachers respond by teaching to the test. But when *students* are being tested, teachers become trainers and mentors. In that environment, teachers are not bureaucratically pressured to pander to students who have no ambition beyond getting a good score. Teachers may still pander, but the test itself will not be a pressure to pander. It will not divert teachers from caring about students into caring about transcripts.

A crucial aspect of our current predicament is that measuring inputs is, as a general rule, counterproductive. When we measure inputs, we are bound to create the wrong incentives. The organization as a whole in effect forgets that what matters is maximizing what customers get *out* of education, not maximizing what investors put *into* it.

Measuring grades and graduation rates is likewise probably counterproductive. It is plausible to suppose that those things correlate to real learning, other things equal. However, if we make grades or graduation rates our target, then other things are not equal. The targeting itself corrupts. There is a saying, "Be careful what you wish for." There could be and should be a correspondingly chilling saying, "Be careful what you measure," with a similar implication.

There may be a correlation between x and y. However, trying to measure that correlation could be the very thing that breaks the connection by transforming the signal into the objective.

ACCOUNTABILITY

Measurement is a problem. Because measurement is a problem, teachers teaching to the test is a problem. We do not want a system of competition that does little more than induce teaching to the test. Pretend competition induces pretend excellence. If we want a system of education that puts students in a position to know how to flourish, we will need to do better than faux competition, faux markets, and faux excellence.

At the same time, what we genuinely need to assess is relatively simple in principle: Do teachers care? Do they work at their craft? Do they want to use the best methods available? Do they want feedback? Can they take feedback in stride? Questions like these, however, will not be answered by the kind of tests that distant bureaucrats can administer. The assessment we actually need requires situated judgment—the kind that becomes increasingly impossible as a bureaucracy (whether private or public) expands. Caring does not by itself make for a great teacher. But caring goes a long way, and there is no substitute for it. Distant bureaucrats cannot tell. It is not their fault. The bottom line: When it comes to knowing whether a teacher cares, parents can tell. Other teachers can tell. Students can tell, and students respond. Union bosses and politicians cannot tell; they cannot even be counted on to care. But even if we could count on distant administrators to care, the fact remains that without local information, distant administrators will not know who needs to be honored and who needs to be fired.

CERTIFYING TEACHERS: DANGEROUS SERVANT, TERRIBLE MASTER

In Jal Mehta's opinion, top-down centralization movements were a particular vision of modernity, driven to some extent by the sexism of generations past, when front-line teachers were mostly female and administrators mostly male.[5] Mehta condemns it thus:

> The people we draw into teaching are less than our most talented; we give them short or nonexistent training and equip them with little relevant knowledge; we send many of them to schools afflicted by high levels of poverty and segregation; and when they don't deliver the results we seek, we increase external pressure and accountability, hoping that we can do on the back end what we failed to create on the front end.[6]

In our best schools, people with a passion for excellence are turned loose to get the job done. Perhaps the same can be said of some of our worst schools, except that the people being turned loose are incompetent or worse. The implication, however, is not that we cannot afford to experiment but that we cannot afford *not* to, and that we cannot afford to shy away from taking responsibility for shutting down experiments that aren't working.

The alternative is to bureaucratize and thereby kill both passion and professionalism. It is a truism that when it comes to realizing potential for excellence, schools get more out of teachers and students by expecting more. Successful schools seem to operate according to a particular separation of powers. First, teachers are treated as professionals and given some latitude when it comes to determining content and method. Second, local administrators have the right and the responsibility to evaluate, hire, and fire. Third, students or parents have the power and the right to vote with their feet, and are responsible for knowing when the time has come to look for something better. No one can guarantee that parents will know when it is time to look for alternatives, but it is hard to imagine who would be better than a student, or that student's parents, at knowing when that student needs a better option. In isolation or even in tandem, these three powers cannot guarantee successful education. Still, in concert they tend to add up to a balance of power that gets results.

When it comes to evaluating teachers, we are badly missing the point unless we grasp that it is the parents who have to evaluate teachers. Parents fall down on the job only when they are fooled into thinking that someone else has everything under control. It is the parents who need to take responsibility for being unimpressed by good scores when they can see for themselves that their child has not yet learned to read or add fractions.

REGIMENTATION

How standardized should a curriculum be? We exaggerate the extent to which every child needs to study the same stuff so as to become mutually intelligible fellow citizens. We need not practice the same religion to be mutually intelligible. Neither do we need a common curriculum.

A less obvious reason for a common curriculum is to regiment the task of holding *teachers* accountable and thus to make it unnecessary to rely on situated judgment and the wisdom of local administrators. But consider how counterproductive it would be to work from a premise that no current or future teacher will ever have better ideas than the ideas currently in vogue among distant bureaucrats appointed on the basis of political connections. Teachers on the ground regularly discover better material and better methods. Sometimes the best we can do to help is to stay out of the way.

What distinguishes trusting politicians from trusting highly motivated and relatively well-situated buyers and sellers to make decisions that shape our schools? The difference is not that we don't get mistakes if we go the political route; it's that we don't get small mistakes. We get big mistakes, and we get bureaucrats who are more eager to cover up mistakes than to correct them.

Mehta describes President George W. Bush's No Child Left Behind Act as the third major attempt (the Progressive Era and the 1960s being the first two) to institute accountability for education from the top down. Mehta's sad conclusion, announced at the outset, is that

> there is no sign that the reforms have had a significant impact in closing achievement gaps or in improving America's mediocre international educational standing. Particularly in the most troubled schools, there has been rampant teaching to the test and some outright cheating. In-depth studies have shown that some schools now devote a large part of their year to test prep; Atlanta and D[istrict of] C[olumbia] public

schools have both contended with widespread cheating scandals. There are substantial concerns that simplistic testing is crowding out richer forms of learning.[7]

Referring to the centralizing movement as it began in the Progressive Era, Mehta writes:

Then, as now, teachers charged that such movements were wrongly applying the logic of industry to schools and argued that education had a deeper "bottom line."[8]

Mehta's diagnosis of the failing common to all three reform movements is that in each case, what resulted was a mindless regimen of quantification. All three movements sought to reduce variation among schools. All three exhibited an outsized faith in scientific management, failing to acknowledge the extent to which excellence in teaching requires artistry, somewhat as does excellence in acting.[9] Teaching also is reducible to a science *to some extent*, in the same way if not to the same degree that excellence in medicine is. As with medicine, though, teaching requires skill and discretion, not just rules and procedures.

In the 1980s, Mehta says, "state after state began to use standards, assessments, and accountability as the linked technology for improvement from afar."[10] Mehta also says the union movement of the 1960s institutionalized teachers as labor rather than as professionals. But teaching is "complex and requires significant skill and discretion"; that is to say, it cannot be routinized in the manner of union labor. "The core of the education problem is that we have been trying to solve a problem of professional practice by bureaucratic means."[11]

What today is called Common Core is a real problem. It is also a response to a real problem—namely, that there has to be accountability in the system. If there has to be accountability, then there has to be evaluation. But how to introduce forms of accountability that do not make things worse? That is a question to which I have no answer. The debate over nationally driven Common Core standards is not a partisan issue in any obvious way. It is the sort of thing conservatives favor in principle. It was introduced by a Republican president. But currently it is liberals who hesitantly back it, while conservatives seem to regard it as an illegitimate federal power grab.

Why, Mehta asks, despite modest results, has so much (bipartisan) political energy gone into regimenting schools?[12] The reason is that we want to subject *teachers* to standardized tests. But however well motivated that drive to centralize the evaluation of teachers may be, it seems not to work. Perhaps there is a consensus that schools are so important that something needs to be done—regardless of whether that something solves the problem, and indeed regardless of whether there is any actual problem. Perhaps there also is a consensus that schools are so important that we cannot let them be laboratories. Letting them be laboratories would be playing God. Though it may seem intelligible to recoil from the prospect of taking responsibility for our experiments, the result is that we end up playing God so as to avoid an *appearance* of playing God. We pretend we do not need to learn, and pretend we do not need to experiment, in order to find out what works.

That is what is unforgivable. We end up trying to prove that no matter how much damage we do, our heart is in the right place. People who say we cannot risk making mistakes with children's lives are so often the same people willing to bet whole countries on untested theories. They say we cannot play God with children's lives; so we play God with a hundred million lives at a time.

Elizabeth Anderson observes that in some cases,

> impersonal rule-of-law regulations impose constraints so out of touch with local conditions, with such draconian penalties for noncompliance, that enforcement amounts to domination. Such is the case with the high-stakes testing regime imposed by the Federal Government under No Child Left Behind, with uniform arbitrary progress goals foisted on local school districts without any empirical research demonstrating that these goals were feasible. In some cases, the NCLB regime has created a culture of intimidation and cheating. This is a centralized planning regime akin to the five-year plans of communist states.[13]

MEASURING UP

What if what we truly want isn't measurable?

Great teachers look their students in the eye. When students look back, they see a reflection—not what they are, mind you, but what the teacher expects them to become. They step up. Why? Partly because they do not want to disappoint the teacher, but mainly because they are learning what to expect from themselves.

What can a society do to make a teacher feel that it pays to be inspired? Perhaps even more crucially, what can a society do to make students feel that it pays to be inspired? If you think about teachers in your past who made you a better person, my conjecture is: first, they loved what they were teaching, and you could tell; second, they took you aside and said something to you that made you resolve not to disappoint them.

What those teachers knew is not that teachers are the center of the universe; rather, almost the opposite. The characteristic ferocity of an inspired teacher is about learning, not teaching. Real learning is a passion. It is glorious. The passion of an inspired teacher is contagious.

Parents and students need to know how important it is to provide feedback to teachers who achieve that greatness. Feedback is no substitute for an adequate salary, but it is crucial to sustaining a culture of professional pride. Parents and students can inspire in turn, tracking down teachers who deserve to be told, "Hey, teacher, it has not escaped us that you go the extra mile, and that *your* class is the class where our child is stepping it up a notch, and you are the teacher that our kid refuses to disappoint."

We all grew up with a mixed bag of teachers, but most of us can remember a few teachers who inspired, and that was enough. We remember one or two who took us aside and said, more or less gently, "You've got something in you, and you have no right to not aim high." We needed to hear that. Students still need to hear it today. If we recall from our own experience, what we remember about teachers at their best is that they *care*. They care about how well a child is doing, not how well a child is scoring.

When we think about our finest moments as teachers, the truth about those moments is that the job market and assessments were the furthest thing from our minds. Those were the days when we went home pondering a thought like this: *Today, I explained why* Plato's Republic *is one of the peaks of human achievement. My students took off their head-phones, set aside their laptops, and listened. Somewhere in that room today, quite possibly, was a kid who heard what he or she needed to hear, about a life worth living, in order to be able to carry on.* Those are the days that make it worth getting up the next morning and trying again.

FOREIGN COMPETITION

It would be good to know which countries are doing better than others, what they are doing better, and which dimensions of their success can be emulated. Or perhaps we need to know whether the sense in which they are doing better is a statistical artifact not worth emulating.

Amanda Ripley finds three differences between the United States and the countries with superior educational performance.[14] First, on Ripley's analysis, students in top American schools and top countries believe that how hard they work and well they do in school will affect how interesting their lives will be. To them, education's purpose is obvious. Moreover, students at high-performing schools are aware that when it comes to running with opportunities that will define their lives, they will not be able to hide behind faux credentials. Their success will depend on how well equipped they are with real skills, not how well credentialed they are. Accordingly, they wake up in the morning aiming to master some skill that they have not yet mastered, a skill that is worth mastering and which cannot be mastered without sustained effort.

The second difference is that in high-performing American schools and in the schools of high-performing countries, school is hard. Top schools have higher standards. They do not shy away from raising standards on the grounds that they cannot accept the risk that not everyone will be able to meet them. The whole point of higher standards is that students have to learn something in order to meet them. High performers accept that if there is no guarantee that every child will pass, then not every child will pass. As Ripley puts it, the problem with American education is that American teachers and administrators are not being honest enough with students about how much better students could do. She says that making colleges of education more selective and more demanding has helped every country that has tried it.

The third factor that separates top countries and top schools from mediocre ones, in Ripley's view, is that in the top schools, sports are a hobby, not a way of life, and not a source of a school's identity. More generally, Ripley says, there is too much distraction in underperforming schools, and one of the more manageable distractions is sports. (Drugs are a problem everywhere; even the best schools in the best countries have not solved that problem.) Ripley does, however, heed a lesson from successful coaches: that great coaches embrace the possibility of failure, and put failure in context. They treat success as attainable. Above all, they teach that hard work pays, including hard work on behalf of goals sufficiently lofty that success, even for the hardest workers, is not guaranteed. Great coaches instill an attitude and a work ethic that makes students stronger. Good students learn that there will be days when they have to come back from defeat.

We may have something to learn, then, from experiments in other countries. However, a word of caution is needed. If Finland is outperforming America along measurable dimensions, there's a way in which *caring might be a mistake*. Joseph Stalin declared in 1945 that the Soviet Union's planned economy would be the world's leading industrial power by 1960. The Soviet Union did in fact ramp up steel production and so on. To what end? Part of the planners' mission was to outproduce economies such as Germany and the United States. But by the late 1950s, when the USSR was indeed a prodigious producer of steel, only a tiny percentage of the steel was going into cars, washing machines, or other consumer goods. John Kennedy, then a senator, speculated that the missing 90 percent must be going into the Soviet military, but he never imagined that the bulk of it might be going into nothing at all. In fact, that steel was being produced in response not to orders placed by customers but to orders issued by planners.

Soviet steel production is among history's best examples of what Marxists disparagingly call production for production's sake. The Soviets meant to be sneering at Western commercialism, but they had it altogether backward. Centrally planned steel mills were producing to win rather than to fill customer orders. They worked to meet quotas, not to meet market demand. Soviet planners drove everyone to produce an appearance of productivity rather than a reality. To see *that* as a model of how to run schools like a business is to think like Soviets. That is the mistake we risk making if we treat education's goal as having to do with outcompeting other nations.

The guiding questions should instead be these: Who wants education? What kind of education do they want? What *should* they want? What exactly are they willing to pay for? What is worth their time and money?

Consider that no one cares whether the United States leads the world in tons of steel produced. We do not even ask. Why not? *Because we know what steel is for.* The point is not to collect the prize for being number one. The point is not to send a signal that the United States is a stellar producer. On the contrary, the point is for particular businesses to satisfy particular customers who have placed particular orders. That form of interaction defines market society.

When I was in Korea, I talked about some of this material. I told the audience that I found it interesting that Korea had one of the world's two top-rated educational systems, yet it is so unlike Finland, the other top country. The students reacted to me with a palpable sense of urgency. They said, "No, you must not say Korea has a great system. It has a terrible system. We in this room are the survivors. We are the winners. We are the advantaged. We have the least complaint of anyone, but we never had childhoods. All we ever did was study. And for what? We are not more creative than Americans or Europeans, who had allegedly inferior educations. We are not more productive. We are just better at conforming, which is not altogether bad and could even be considered a virtue, but it's not enough to justify taking away a person's childhood. We do not want our children to grow up the way that we did." I have never before or since been in a situation like that, surrounded by people who were so anguished, and so concerned to warn the world not treat them as a role model.

OVERSUPPLY?

You can read that in Finland, schoolchildren have fewer classes, shorter classes, less homework, more time for recess. Does that mean children are underworked? Does it mean schools are less important than we think? How much learning goes on after hours?

What, if anything, should we be learning from Finland's example? Perhaps this: If we want learning to be self-directed and self-affirming, we had better let students skirt the edge of boredom. Give students time to invent themselves. Perhaps our students spend too *much* time in class rather than too little, or too much time in classes that do not in fact have a point.

We read that teaching loads are lighter in Finland. Is that good? We strive to get more out of teachers, but when we ask for more hours, more *hours* is what we get, at the expense of teachers having time to think. It is not only students who need time to play. Teachers need time to reflect on where the world needs them to be going forward. Let teachers reflect on which students are worth encouraging in which ways. Do our teachers have time for that?[15]

Can we turn teachers from judges into coaches by having someone external to the class do the grading? The teacher still provides the feedback, but if the teacher is merely a coach and not the judge, jury, and executioner, the relationship becomes simpler. That sounds bureaucratically cumbersome to me, but we might learn something from controlled testing of that model of how to separate the educating from the certifying.

Pasi Sahlberg says Finland has an alternative to market-based reform. Finland limits student testing to a minimum. It places responsibility and trust before accountability.[16] It treats education problems as local problems, more or less, in need of more or less local solutions. I am led to reflect that many things are described as market-based reform; many of them do not work. This will always be true of markets. Markets are sites of experimentation. Market societies (including Finland) are sites where we see new innovation and new art. For precisely that reason, we see prodigious quantities of bad art, and prodigious numbers of failed experiments. Unquestionably, many of the experiments conducted under the banner of totalizing and colonizing efforts like No Child Left Behind have failed. What is the lesson? Should we avoid experimenting? Or instead, should we avoid betting whole countries on the kinds of experiments that government czars undertake? There is a false confidence that comes from knowing that the price of failure will be paid by distant others, nameless and faceless. We might consider how to avoid counting on bureaucrats for whom actual failure has no personal consequence, and the only thing they are anxious to avoid is *evidence* of failure.

To be sure, some failed experiments may have been worth a try. Experimenting may have been the only way to find out. If there was a big mistake, it was simply the thought that experiments have to be run on a national scale. A related mistake is to think that if we find a solution that works in a particular time and place, we should copy it. That is not always true. We should study success and learn whatever lessons a particular success can teach us, but learning from a success is not always about learning how to scale it up.

Another related point: as with bad art, the market does not necessarily presume to tell us that an experiment is failing. Markets let customers choose. If customers are willing to pay for bad art, so be it. We can, of course, imagine customers choosing bad education, too, and being slow to learn that they could do better. A visionary politician might see the mistake earlier and shut down the mistake earlier. Or visionary politicians might be the first to make the mistake and the last to learn from it, as with the many versions of No Child Left Behind adopted over the years with bipartisan support.

I suspect that what Sahlberg calls the Finnish lesson is a lesson from which other countries could learn. Sahlberg calls the Finnish lesson an alternative to market-based reform. True? Perhaps. Or perhaps the Finnish idea is no more and no less than a simple idea that arguably is worth a try. Indeed, perhaps the Finnish model is exactly the kind of idea that markets do try, and the kind of idea that catches fire in a market society if it turns out to be a success.

FINAL THOUGHT

At the end of the day, the morality of being a producer of service X answers to how good it is to be a consumer of X. This aspect of morality is what markets deliver when they are working. We want to believe some other form of organization can mimic this efficiency. We want to believe we can improve upon a logic that is uniquely responsive to consumer demand.

Again, using standardized tests to test *teachers* yields teachers who teach to the test. That is what transforms the signal into the objective. It is like Soviet factories imposing quotas that led to factories producing the appearance of a product rather than anything customers wanted. Factories given quotas measured in number of discrete items produced thumbtacks, whereas factories given quotas measured in tons produced railroad spikes. All were tasked with producing items falling under the general description of "nails" but had no feedback regarding the specific kinds of functionality that customers were paying for.

Inevitably, factories responded efficiently to the quota given, but efficiency in meeting quotas had nothing to do with whether customers had any use for their product. The Soviets had a philosophy. They were not willing to let people respond to each other and figure out how to make each other better off, lest the arc of progress leave their philosophy behind.

Suppose planners were to try to devise a non-market alternative that is more rational, efficient, or compassionate than markets. They would need measures, and standards of accountability. They would have less information than parents would, and could not be presumed to care as much as parents would, but still they would need something. At some point, planners wishing to bypass price signals and consumer sovereignty would have to jump in and design programs to goose some measurable, such as graduation rates, as if outscoring Finland on graduation rates were an end in itself. How would they avoid doing what planners have a history of doing—namely, committing us to waste on a Soviet scale?

What is the gold standard of accountability, by which all other measures of success have been found wanting? How do producers know that a product is worth its cost, other than by taking it to market and finding out whether customers are willing to pay enough to cover cost of making more?

We treat education as good. We think education pays, both intrinsically and instrumentally. But does it pay to know Latin? It depends. Where knowing Latin pays more, we should expect to see people investing more in knowing Latin. Where people invest more, it may be because knowing Latin is worth more there. Where people invest more in education, perhaps it is a sign that education is worth more there. What about Finland? Is education more valuable in Finland than elsewhere? Is demand for education higher in Finland? If so, why? Is there an outsized demand in Finland for highly educated workers? Is there a "Nokia" effect—Finnish technology firms paying top dollar for large numbers of highly skilled workers?

The idea is not absurd. Obviously, the payoff to being highly educated is higher in some places than in others. If people spent less on education in the United States than in Finland, it might be because education is not worth as much in the United States as in Finland. Alternatively, it could be a sign that education is undersupplied in the United States, or oversupplied in Finland. How would we know? Almost all the relevant literature presupposes that quality education is undersupplied in the United States.

The presumption seems plausible, at least when it comes to educating the poorest of the poor and historically disadvantaged minorities, but why would education be undersupplied in the United States? What is preventing markets in education from operating as markets normally operate?[17] If the demand for quality education, delivered in a cost-effective way, is strong in the United States, and if manifest demand is not being met, *why aren't suppliers stepping up to meet it*?

NOTES

1. Derek Neal, "The Consequences of Using One Assessment System to Pursue Two Objectives," *Journal of Economic Education* 44 (2013): 339.
2. See Alan Blinder, "Atlanta Educators Convicted in School Cheating Scandal," *New York Times*, April 1, 2015.
3. Jal Mehta, *The Allure of Order* (New York: Oxford University Press, 2013), 8–9.
4. Mehta, *The Allure of Order*, 260.
5. Mehta, *The Allure of Order*, 40–41.
6. Mehta, *The Allure of Order*, 7.
7. Mehta, *The Allure of Order*, 1–2.
8. Mehta, *The Allure of Order*, 3.
9. Mehta, *The Allure of Order*, 4, 5.
10. Mehta, *The Allure of Order*, 12.
11. Mehta, *The Allure of Order*, 270.
12. Mehta, *The Allure of Order*, 48.
13. Elizabeth Anderson, "Freedom and Equality," in *Oxford Handbook of Freedom*, ed. David Schmidtz and Carmen Pavel (New York: Oxford University Press, 2018), 92.
14. Amanda Ripley, *The Smartest Kids in the World* (New York: Simon & Schuster, 2013).
15. Ripley notes that South Korea and Finland are equally stellar in terms of educational achievement, but South Korea emphasizes putting in the hard work more than any other country, to a point where observers cannot help wondering whether investing a child's every waking hour in education is worth the personal cost. Ripley, *The Smartest Kids in the World*, ch. 3.
16. See Pasi Sahlberg, *Finnish Lessons: What Can the World Learn from Educational Change in Finland?* (New York: Teacher's College Press, 2016), 6.
17. In the short term, the fact that education is expensive is obviously relevant, but when computers were so expensive in the 1960s that only the military could afford them, entrepreneurs aimed to get the cost down to where

computers were affordable to children. When mobile phones first appeared in the 1980s at a cost of around $4,000, entrepreneurs aimed to get the cost down to where mobile phones were affordable to children. Schools have been around for a lot longer than computers and cellphones. Why isn't the cost dropping? Or is this the wrong question?

3

Society Is Not a Race

THEME: WE OBSERVED THAT EDUCATORS AND educational institutions have a twofold mission. Here is an implication: If we perform well in our role as educators, we make our classroom a *society*—a cooperative venture for mutual advantage. If we perform well as certifiers, we turn our classroom into something else: a *race*, albeit a fair one.

What is the difference between a society and a race? First, when one literally is racing, it is fine for the fact of being *fast* to be a negative for those against whom one is competing.

Second, in a race, there is a reason for people to start on an equal footing. A race's purpose is to measure relative performance. So, equal opportunity is absolutely to the point in actual races. Why? Because in an actual race, the point is to sort people in terms of their realized excellences. Therefore, we want the fact of finishing first to indicate having run the fastest; we want it to indicate excellence. We want excellence to be a *telling* advantage. The point of the race requires that the relative excellence of competitors not be gratuitously obscured by advantages not relevant to the particular excellence that our race was meant to measure.

By contrast, a society's purpose, insofar as a society can be said to have a purpose, is not to measure relative performance but to be a good place to live. To be a good place to live, a society needs to be a place where people do not face arbitrary bias or exclusion. In liberal society at its best, women and men, blacks and whites, regardless of religion, have a chance to live well (and realize their potential to make the world better) as free and responsible citizens.

Here is another way to express the difference. In a race, we win by making others lose. In a society, we flourish by helping others flourish.

Therefore, first, that is why in a society we want citizens to have a good footing. Second, that also is why the question of whether citizens have an *equal* footing does not matter in the same way that it would matter in a race.

We are political animals and social animals who win by making others glad we were here—glad we showed up. In games where one person's success comes at no one else's expense (including the game of learning something), no one needs everyone to have the same potential. No student needs everyone to develop their potential to the same level. No student needs every child's education to be equally effective at developing potential. We do not even know what it would mean for every education to be equally effective. We do not need to know. The exact thing students need, no more and no less, is a genuine chance to make something of whatever potential they have.

In short, society is not a race. No one needs to win. Therefore, no one needs an equal chance to win.

LIFE CHANCES: A
ZERO-SUM PERSPECTIVE

For people born years apart, in tangibly different circumstances, the idea of literally equal life chances (along every dimension in which life's value might be measured) is not even meaningful. How so? Here is my thinking.

First, each of us is born into a world teeming with opportunities that exist in part because people have been taking advantage of opportunities since before we were born—taking advantage of opportunities in such a way as to expand the frontier of possibility, creating new opportunities wherever we look.

Second, as mentioned, some people are more skilled than others simply because they were born earlier and started practicing earlier. A society that worked to ensure that extra skills and experience are *not* a competitive advantage would be a monstrous failure as a society.

Third, everyone would like to see a society in which sex, race, or skin color is not in general a disadvantage. Every liberal wants to live in a society where the caste into which you are born does not define your life chances. We might wish it did not matter whether your parents have resources with which to help you, or whether your parents care about you. We might *say* we wish it did not matter. But realistically, such things matter, and will continue to matter so long as anything at all matters. Such factors lead us toward a society where opportunities are good, but not so much toward a society in which opportunities are equal.

Most people, when asked, would casually agree that life was better in the old days. But people who actually look see opportunities expanding. They might even see a playing field becoming more level in ways that matter most to the least advantaged.[1] But there will never be a day when we find that different people's opportunities have been made identical. There will never be a day when that kind of equality is what we actually want. Even if it matters in some way that opportunities be identical, it cannot matter in the way it matters whether opportunities are good. It cannot matter in the way that it matters whether opportunities are improving.

The ultimate fairness is living in a world where other people becoming capable is a good thing, not a bad thing. The legitimate egalitarian dream is not making it impossible for others to "get ahead" so much as making it true that others getting ahead is not a threat. We want to live in a world where getting an education is something we all celebrate. We want to live in a world where other people's good luck is a good thing, not a bad thing. We want neighbors to be people we root for, not against. The ideal has nothing to do with learning how to prevent other people succeeding and everything to do with learning not to resent other people succeeding. The ideal is to have (and learn that we have) no reason to see other people as threats, and every reason to see their burgeoning capacities as a triumph for all.

CUMULATIVE EFFECTS

Naturally, by the time students get to our college classrooms, they are products of their previous education. There are butterfly effects.[2] Differences in opportunity accumulate, and they coalesce into differences in talent and differences in reward. The effects conceivably could multiply over generations. Some see this as a moral problem, leading to hierarchical class structure and a crumbling of any semblance of equal opportunity.

The premise of cumulative benefits is itself premised on an idea that the educational system *works*. How bad can that problem be? (Could anything cure this problem without being worse than the disease?) It would be damning if it did not matter whether a person's previous education was good or bad.

A good education had better be an advantage, hopefully an advantage that further education can magnify and perpetuate. If some educations are too good, then something outside the educational system needs fixing. In particular, if educated people systematically are turning to piracy to make a living, something has gone wrong with society as a whole, not with education per se. (I am not here denying the obvious: namely, if you were a teacher and you saw that you were working to turn your students into better pirates, that would be good reason to quit.)

Cumulative advantages might seem unfair if education's purpose were to prepare students to compete in zero-sum games. But if instead our hope as citizens is to deal with excellent plumbers, excellent teachers, and so on, then we want advantages not only for ourselves but also for everyone with whom we deal. We want the people with whom we deal to be good at what they do. We do not need to be *compensated* for having to be operated on by virtuoso surgeons. We compensate *them* for developing skills that may someday save our lives, and for bringing such excellence to market in the hope of making the world a better place.

To be clear, my co-author would correctly stress that we cannot talk realistically about equal opportunity within schools without acknowledging that what is outside the schools is not "all else equal." Everyone, including me, should heed that warning. To me, the compelling egalitarian ideal is to do everything we can to prepare children for adulthood, one child at a time. The compelling egalitarian ideal is to regard every child as innocent, and to regard every child as needing, deserving, and ideally actually getting our best shot at helping that child be what that child can be.[3]

But we cannot escape responsibility for asking ourselves, when we educate elites, are we preparing them to be excellent contributors? Or excellent pirates? I presume the former. However, that really is a presumption on my part, and whether that presumption is true is a highly relevant empirical contingency. That presumption is at the heart of whether we are living in a just society. There have been times and places where it was not true. But that is to say there is a bigger picture of which education is one part. Whether a system of education is serving the cause of justice can depend on broader variables that do not have much to do with schools.

I brood over the following fact: Every year, tens of thousands of middle schoolers in inner city schools across the United States get standardized-test results suggesting they have genius potential. Then, within a few years, most of those young souls seemingly disappear, never to be heard from again. They get on with whatever teenagers have to do to survive the ghetto.

I did not grow up in a ghetto. I grew up on a farm, but we were poor. (I remember when we got our first flush toilet.) There are many reasons why I was able to move from near the bottom of North America's income distribution to near the top. However, I can say with certainty that high on the list of reasons for my success were successive strokes of pure luck.

LEARNING THAT COOPERATION IS POSITIVE-SUM

Many thinkers in the liberal tradition have accepted that for literacy to be maximally justified, people in general, not only literate people in particular, have to be better off in literate society. And of course, they are.

More subtly, for society's sake, students must *learn* that they are better off in a literate society; therefore, teaching students to be fit for citizenship goes beyond merely giving them tools of basic literacy. Students also must acquire particular skills and commitments involved in successful cooperation. Students must learn that the game for which they are being prepared is a positive-sum game in which a winning performance should be good for people in general, not only for the winning performer in particular. Thus, one of the greatest favors we do for gifted students is to actively encourage them to tutor their classmates, and thereby achieve a depth of understanding that students cannot achieve by passively listening.

People should *know* they are better off when their classmates grow up to be better surgeons, engineers, executives, legislators, journalists, and teachers. If they are better off, then the fact that their classmates grew up needing to compete for market share is not in any serious way a negative. Crucially, if a rising tide of excellence is not a negative, then neither is the fact that some people had advantages in their quest to get better at doing what they do best.[4]

Egalitarianism cannot survive inspection as a call for enforcing a static pattern (e.g., of income shares), but that is not what liberal egalitarianism is. The point of the liberal ideal of political equality is not to *stop* us from becoming more worthy along dimensions where our worth can be affected by our choices, but to *facilitate* our becoming more worthy.

JUSTICE AS DIVIDING THE PIE VERSUS JUSTICE AS RESPECTING BAKERS

Traditional liberals wanted people—all people—to be as free as possible to pursue their dreams. Accordingly, the liberal tradition of equal opportunity put the emphasis on improving opportunities, not on equalizing them. Within the nineteenth-century tradition from which the ideal of "equal pay for equal work" emerged, that aspiration had more in common with meritocracy, and with the equal respect embodied by meritocracy, than with equal shares per se.

Liberal political equality is not premised on the absurd hope that, under ideal conditions, we all turn out to be equally worthy. It presupposes only a traditionally liberal optimism regarding what kind of society results from giving everyone, so far as we can, a chance to choose worthy ways of life. We do not see people's different contributions as equally valuable, but that was never the point of equal opportunity and never could be.

Why not? *Because we do not see even our own contributions to society as equally worthy, let alone everyone's.* We are not indifferent to whether we achieve more rather than less. Some of our efforts have excellent results. Some do not. We can tell the difference, and we care about it. In everyday life, genuine respect tracks how we distinguish ourselves as we develop our unique potentials in unique ways.

The intuitive case for educational equality rests on an intuition about what it takes for a competition to be fair.[5] The intuition is that society is a race. As an intuition, it is powerful, pervasive, compelling—something we have believed since we were toddlers. But primeval though this intuition seems to be, it does not start at the start. It assumes we compete for a pie that sits there like a prize to be awarded to the winner of a race. Is it fair to ignore the fact that the pie exists because of histories of productive effort? To me, it seems manifestly fair to ask "What made this pie yours to distribute?" *before* we ask "What way of distributing it would be fair, given that it is yours to distribute?"

I get the intuition that there should be some kind of level playing field. I get the intuition that society is a race, even though I think this intuition is in fact a cognitive bias that has no utility, is not descriptively accurate, and is one that we do well to outgrow. At issue is not merely how to balance equality against, say, parental autonomy, but which dimensions of equality are defensible as elements of justice that we must balance against parental autonomy.

Assigning the poorest kids to the worst public schools does not lead to equal opportunity. To say the poorest kids should be educated in public schools pays lip service to equal opportunity, but none of us has any right to be satisfied with lip service. Maybe we do have a way of equalizing opportunity that the least advantaged have reason to endorse. But identifying that option would be hard empirical work.

EQUALITY TO WIN

I have seen a bumper sticker that says, "The only person you should be trying to be better than is the person you were yesterday." The sentiment is clear enough. In real life, self-improvement generally serves a purpose, and keeping up with (or beating) the Joneses generally does not. Leveling down egalitarianism—shackling the Joneses to make sure that keeping up with them is not a challenge—would be counterproductive in the extreme. Thus, almost no egalitarian today explicitly endorses leveling down.

Brighouse and Swift say, "Of course, society is indeed not a race. But *our* society is *relevantly like* a race." What do they mean? Their next sentence continues: "The distribution of the benefits of social cooperation is structured to reward those who do well and penalize those who do badly in competitions they have no feasible alternative to participating in."[6] Speaking as sole author, Brighouse says, "Whether someone achieves high status or income depends not just on their own talents and what they do with them, but on the design of the social institutions they are lucky, or unlucky, enough to inhabit. Consider the remarkable incomes that top sports players earn in contemporary developed societies; the talents they have developed command the rewards they do for many contingent reasons for which they can claim no credit."[7]

There is a lot going on here. It will not be easy to unpack. However, the sentiments are so nearly universal that it is worth trying. First, the general story to which Brighouse and Swift allude is so well known that they do not bother to elaborate, but the basic idea is that everyone has genes, and everyone has an upbringing that they did not cause and for which they deserve no credit. This story's beginning is, far too conveniently, also the end. The story of how we deserve is over before it can start. Because bakers are a mere *result*, we need not respond to the pies they bring to the table as if the bakers deserve some credit for bringing them.

This sort of move is so familiar to philosophers that we no longer recoil from it. Instead, we learn to ignore how such moves hollow out the whole idea of individual agency. According to the narrative that goes with this move, we acknowledge the reality and individuality of demand, consumption, and interests, but we avert our gaze from the reality and individuality of supply. Instead, we credit supply to society as a whole. We avert our gaze from the dynamic and highly contingent history of what bakers go through to get their pies to the table.

Does the fact that I have a history limit how much credit I can deserve for whatever I bring to the table? (Would that mean members of my support group deserve more credit for what I bring to the table, or less? After all, they too have a history.) Does the bare fact of being a situated social animal make me undeserving?

Can we be certain that any randomly selected person is undeserving? Does the bare fact that a person is a person guarantee that the person is undeserving? Does living in a world with a history, a world of cause and effect, guarantee that we are all undeserving? Can we be certain without needing to know any contingent facts about what a given person has done? Yes, to judge by the general thrust of contemporary philosophical commentary on the topic of desert. But that kind of work *aspires* to make the concept of desert useless.

My view is that if our conception of desert is insensitive to contingency—if our conception *aspires* to be useless in sorting people out— then we need to go back to square one and come up with a non-spurious conception of desert. We need a conception that can sort people out on the basis of what people observably bring to the table. Situated talent is out there in the world, observably instantiated in flesh-and-blood individuals. No doubt the existence of such potential for excellence is caused, but the issue is not whether potential is caused but whether it is real.

Talent is real. Opportunities to develop talent are real. There are respectful and constructive ways of responding to these realities.

THE MERITOCRATIC CONCEPTION

The idea of meritocracy, as Brighouse and Swift characterize it, is the idea that an individual's prospects for educational achievement may be a function of that individual's talent and effort, but her prospects should not be influenced by her social class background.[8] Their conclusion is plausible. My concern is not that their conclusion is false so much as that it is not an idea of meritocracy.

The idea is that departures from equality can be justified by merit. Maybe so, but it is egalitarianism, not meritocracy, that treats departing from equality as what needs justifying. Genuine principles of merit are theories about how to respond to excellence, not how to respond to departures from equality.[9]

What Brighouse and Swift are challenging here is the tying of rewards to class background. I have no quarrel with that. We can agree about the dubiousness of rewarding class background. All I would add is that rejecting class-based rewards because they depart from equality is ordinary Rawlsian egalitarianism, not meritocracy. Not that I disagree; on the contrary, I endorse this egalitarian intuition. It too is part of the historical heart of liberalism.

But my point here is that a merit-based theory rejects rewards tied to class background. Why? Because rewards based on class background depart from *merit*, not because they depart from *equality*.[10]

ZERO-SUM

I quoted Brighouse and Swift, and Brighouse writing as sole author. Adam Swift, likewise writing as sole author, considers a hypothetical proposal. Suppose we give parents more freedom to invest whatever resources they have available to educate their kids. What happens next? Swift asks, are poor kids, whose parents cannot afford to invest more,

> as well off as they were before? Of course not. The very fact that the rich kids now have a better chance of success means that the poor kids have a worse one. The new policy doesn't simply give them a worse chance than that enjoyed by the rich kids. It gives them a worse chance than they had before the policy was introduced. In that sense, because of the competitive aspect, chances of achieving scarce goods are zero sum. If some have more, others must have less. So stopping some getting better chances than others is not leveling down. It is not merely cutting down the tall poppies for its own sake. It is positively benefitting those who would otherwise be worse off.[11]

Here, too, the sentiments that Swift articulates are so widespread that they demand attention. Is it an empirical claim that preventing advantaged kids from doing better positively benefits disadvantaged kids? Is Swift saying the claim is true? Does he think there is evidence for it? It may sound like it. However, Swift is not presenting this as a claim needing to be backed up by statistics. What he is actually saying is that the "leveling down" objection has ignored a point of *logic*. That is, as a point of logic, "parents who buy their children an education that gives them a competitive advantage are worsening the prospects of other people's children."[12] Once Swift notes that his world, by definition, is one where opportunities are zero-sum, we are supposed to be embarrassed to have overlooked the obvious problem.

My own view is that we can specify, empirically, exactly when Swift would be right and when he would be wrong. Swift is correct when, but only when, a scarce good genuinely is zero-sum in the sense that the winner's gain is the loser's loss. That is what Swift has in mind. When the good in question is that one precious remaining slot available for admission to medical school, then Swift is right. Suppose two candidates remain for that last slot: one is a disadvantaged poor kid, the other is an advantaged rich kid. If the poor kid's chance of gaining that last slot, in competition with the rich kid, were 10 percent, and if we could raise the poor kid's chance to 50 percent by requiring that admission decisions be made by flipping a coin, then that disadvantaged kid's chances would be higher in a specifiable way. A poor kid loses that benefit when admissions become more sensitive to the advantages of individual candidates. The point of all this is to be clear that I have no quarrel with Swift here. I concede the point, so far as it goes.

What needs to be considered, then, is whether the good in question, admission to medical school, is what matters. What if the genuinely scarce good is the medical training, not the admission? What if every member of society, regardless of where he or she is in the pecking order, has an utterly *overwhelming* interest in society using whatever resources are available to train the best surgeons it can? Swift asks, "How serious are the costs suffered by others if we let parents go private and how many endure the costs?"[13] It we treat this as an empirical question, then the question is fair and to the point. If costs are detectable—suppose they show up as tangible declines in life expectancy, infant mortality, or lifetime income—then they do indeed count for something. But Swift's next sentence suggests that his question is not an empirical question after all, for it turns out that, for him, the beginning of an answer is this: "I've hinted at the downside in terms of unfair inequalities of opportunity suffered by those left behind in the state sector."[14] Swift refers to unfair inequality as an "observation." On the contrary, this is no more an observation than is unfair *equality*. If I were to observe life expectancy rising across the board, that would be a real observation. In that case, I would have a non-theory-laden reason to celebrate: not because the increase is fair but because the increase is an increase.

The flavor of egalitarianism that comes through in the passage from Swift is, I suspect, the very egalitarianism that Swift said he was aiming *not* to defend. The egalitarianism we all endorse is an equal opportunity that minimizes the influence of genuinely *irrelevant* features (sex, race, presumably religion, and so on, when it comes to evaluating people as candidates for medical training). But consider that applicants who have had better learning opportunities all along often will have *relevant* advantages, earned or not. Tracking relevant advantages is the uncontested point of the admissions process. We rely on our system of education to *build on* relevant advantages.

The problem with excluding people on the basis of irrelevant features is that such exclusion squanders opportunities to build on relevant ones. Societies make progress to the extent that they prioritize developing potential wherever potential can be found. When *irrelevant* disadvantages compromise a society's ability to nurture the potential of its next generation, Swift would be absolutely right to say society is to that extent failing.

DOES MERIT TRICKLE DOWN?

Whether permitting parents to pay for private schooling benefits the less advantaged depends on several factors. For example, it depends on whether the gain in human capital to the privileged children yielded by private schooling exceeds any loss to public school students that is caused by the absence of the advantaged children from public schools.

One of Brighouse's concerns is about trickle-down within schools. He believes in trickle-down to the extent of surmising that it is a real advantage of traditional public schools that we could lose if we allow gifted students to be, in effect, segregated. Brighouse is worrying that hothousing gifted students could be costly to students who otherwise would benefit from the presence of those gifted students.[15]

Is Brighouse right? Upon reflection, I am persuaded that he is. In other areas of life, I admit, it is obvious that people find excellence inspiring. Why wouldn't that be as true in classrooms as anywhere else? Again, something I see in my own classroom is that, given the proper coaching, excellent students find it inspiring to discover that they have learned enough to be able to help classmates. So, yes, there may well be a cost to creating separate tracks for gifted students. Merit may well trickle down under the right circumstances. I see it in domains I know best, so if Brighouse sees the same thing in a domain that he knows best, I had better concede the point.

There is a related idea, however, that I would reject: namely, we might imagine that a further cost of hothousing excellent students is that they become dangerously excellent. (If the larger truth about society as a whole were that advantaged kids become parasites, and our teaching had the effect of training them to be more effective as parasites, then education would not be an honorable profession in that society.) Education is on its strongest moral ground in positive-sum societies, that is, societies where gifted students go on to become gifted surgeons, gifted engineers—in a word, gifted contributors. Education is supposed to be good for gifted students, and good for everyone by virtue of being good for gifted students—with benefits that ripple through a society in an empirically obvious way.

As to what is actually good for the least advantaged and what is actually good for gifted children, it takes moral science to answer that question, not just moral philosophy. I admire Brighouse for his leadership on both fronts. In any Western society I know of, when life expectancy of gifted children rises, so does everyone else's. We can, and many of us do, live in societies where what is good for the least advantaged is good for all. But an equally important contingent truth is that we live in societies where what is good for gifted children tends to be good for all.

EQUALITY IN THEORY AND PRACTICE

Few contexts call for thoroughgoing equality as a principle of distribution. In part, this is because so many conceptions of equality that we honor in theory are, in practice, far too complicated compared to familiar alternatives. In practice, it turns out that it is simpler for people to operate by a rule of "What you bring to the table (so long as no other individual can claim to be the one who brought it instead) is presumptively yours, and what other people freely consent to pay you for your service becomes yours once you accept their offer." It is simpler for people to operate by a rule of "You were here first; you go ahead." Many kinds of equalization are not effective in managing traffic or in minimizing analogues of "road rage." And part of the reason why is that they are far simpler in theory than in practice.

A *simple* illustration:

> BIRTHDAY: *"Hey, honey, aren't you enjoying Billy's birthday party?"*
> *"Daddy, how come Billy got a bike and I didn't?"*
> *"Oh, Cindy. Let me give you a hug. It's Billy's eighth birthday, honey. You'll get a bike too, just like his, on your*

*eighth birthday. I promise. But you're only six years old. You
have to wait a bit."*
Cindy pushed away. "Daddy, you're supposed to treat
us the same. If you give Billy a bike, you give me a bike.
And if he gets his now, I get mine now."

What counts as giving six-year-old Cindy an equal
share: giving her a bicycle now, or giving it to her on her
eighth birthday? Can an egalitarian tell Cindy she has to
wait? (Of course, if we give Cindy a bike now, her brother
will have had to wait two years longer than she did. Equality
along one dimension is inequality along another.) So, what
matters from an egalitarian perspective: That we all get our
turn? That we get our turn *at the same time*?

In other words, do equal shares need to *look* like equal
shares at any given moment? Suppose twenty-year-old
Smith is hired today at a wage half that of his forty-year-
old colleague Jones, yet twice what Jones was paid when
Jones was hired twenty years earlier. Does one of them
have a valid complaint? *Which one?* If neither has a valid
egalitarian complaint on its face, the sobering implication is that valid egalitarian complaints are actually quite
sophisticated, and have less to do with *looking* like equals
(from a child's perspective) than we might have thought.[16]

The point is that even if we were to agree that people
should have equal shares, we would remain a long way from
agreeing on what people should have. People can and would
disagree (sometimes reasonably, sometimes childishly)
about what on the surface appears to be a straightforward
factual question regarding whether Billy's and Cindy's
shares are equal.

If helping students to develop their potential is required by justice, then relevant justice is not egalitarian justice. If it is justice, it is justice of some other kind. A school's job is to develop talent, not equalize it. Developing talent is not about comparing slices of pie. Rather, each child is a special case. To be a real teacher is to measure success one student at a time.

I have no quarrel with the idea that every student should be treated as an equal. And we can know what equal treatment means in practice even if we have no idea what it means in theory. I also agree that it is crucial that children learn that they live among peers whom they need to treat as equals. Every parent understands that children need to see adult models of practical impartiality. Children need explanations, too. They dream up stories about how they are not getting their share, so they need to learn that there always are other valid ways of understanding what is going on. Our job as teachers is not to compare what we invest in one child to what we invest in another, but to compare what we invest in a child to what *that child* needs.

When you work with a given student, the time to say "enough" is either when that child is capable of handling it from there or when another student is more in need. Either way, the serious question is about what children *need*, not about what makes them equal.[17]

THE REAL CHALLENGE

The moral imperative can't be to *equalize* effects of education, and realistically that is not an option. Moreover, to restate the obvious, putting students on *identical* footing is out of the question. Even siblings raised in the same house typically have strikingly different opportunity sets (to a point where resentment of siblings is among the most common plot lines in our literature on the human condition). So if in giving students equal opportunity, we are not even *trying* to give them something literally equal, exactly what are we trying to do?

The compellingly important moral challenge is to build a society where education's effects do not need to be equal to be good—a society where success is not a threat. The imperative isn't to equalize education's effects but to structure the system so that education's effects don't need to be equal to be mutually advantageous.

If you want a flourishing society, don't equalize. Instead, make inequality non-threatening.

This challenge is not trivial. There is nothing automatic about education being a public good. On the contrary, it is an achievement, not a given, that a society educates talented people in a way that prepares them to pour their creative energy into inventing ways of making the people around them better off.

It is a further achievement, by no means a given, to enable people to see the difference between having reason to celebrate success and having reason to feel threatened by it. Our egalitarian intuitions can beguile us into mistakenly seeing our world in zero-sum terms. Philosophizing about distributive justice often seems guided by an intuition that we can't get more than an equal share unless someone else gets less than an equal share.

Of course, this intuition is correct, indeed logically necessary. And yet the intuition is also catastrophically misleading, for it suggests that *shares* are what really matter—that distributing rather than producing is the arena where a society's progress takes place or fails to take place. If the pie is expanding, our slice can grow in absolute terms even while our percentage shrinks. In case this seems unlikely, consider that when a population doubles, average share in percentage terms is cut in half. *Necessarily* cut in half. Yet it does not follow, and is not historically true, that average share shrinks in absolute terms as population rises.

In some sense the most obvious fact about society is that voluntary cooperation is mutually advantageous. People voluntarily consummate trades only when they each see the trade as an improvement. If we see people walking out of a corner store having bought a tube of toothpaste for $2, we'll seldom be wrong to infer that they'd rather have the toothpaste than the $2, or that the seller would rather have the $2 than the toothpaste with which he or she started.

One small but important idea about how to make inequality nonthreatening: sometimes, stratifying the classroom is better for all if it can be done without stigma, as when our best students transcend being mere students and take responsibility for tutoring their classmates.

We cannot eliminate all inequality and would not want to try, on pain of becoming a grossly illiberal society. Everyone is an adequacy theorist in practice—that is, someone who says what matters is not whether everyone has the same but whether everyone has enough. We all say "good enough" at some point regardless of any other standard we may officially profess.

WHEN TO EQUALIZE

Suppose we ask: When should schools equalize? That is a bit like asking when plumbers should equalize. The point is not that plumbers are forbidden to equalize but that equalizing is not their job. (Chapter 4 explores this claim.) As with teachers, a plumber's job is to figure out what needs doing, not what makes customers equal. We want each child to have a chance to be as good as that child can be. That is as far as egalitarian educational justice can go. Perhaps there is another kind of justice that goes further in the direction of equalizing. For our purposes, however, that does not matter, because that other kind of justice—in the larger polis—does not regulate the details of education any more than it regulates the details of plumbing.

Here is a caveat, or perhaps a possible inconsistency in my own thinking about this issue. I denied that it is a school's job to equalize, even when equalizing is part of a larger society's job. Yet I do see a role for schools in enabling children to assimilate into their society's larger culture. Why? There are many things I could say, but honestly, I am not sure. I think it is for parents to decide whether aspects of their culture deserve preservation, then choose accordingly: where to live, where to school their children, and what to teach their children at home. I think schools should avoid isolation, division, and "othering" and should instead prepare children to help make their whole community a better place. That will involve preparing them to decide for themselves when preserving their heritage counts as a way of making their community a better place.

A final ambiguity worth noting is this. When people speak of the ideal of a level playing field, they sometimes speak as if leveling the playing field would increase the chance that the game will end in a tie, or as if the only evidence we could have that the playing field is level would consist of seeing games end in a tie. But none of that is true. *A level playing field makes it more likely that the best team wins, not that all teams end up being equally good.*

EQUALITY WITHIN THE REALM OF THE MEASURABLE

Here is a related problem. If we try too hard to make sure we treat everyone equally, we end up looking within the realm of measurable. We look at dimensions of *measurable* equality. When we look for equality of measurables, we end up trying to make sure the *input* we invest in one school equals the input we invest in another. That is a mistake, like trying to measure progress on a long trip by looking at increasing miles from origin rather than at decreasing miles from destination.

Harry Brighouse stresses that a principle of educational meritocracy does not support equality of educational inputs.[18] This is a good, empirically realistic point. Institutions that fail to economize on inputs are disasters waiting to happen. Maintaining a level of input (say, a school budget) is unjustified except in service of maintaining a level of output.

Things can go badly wrong when we treat inputs as the currency of value. Inputs are supposed to translate straightforwardly into outputs, but when we treat measurable inputs as the holy grail, the very process of measuring itself obliterates the connection. The corruption of the signal is lawlike rather than accidental. In that case, goal-directedness is not merely directed but redirected. We end up forgetting that what matters is maximizing what we get out of education, not maximizing what we put into it.

Brighouse and Swift wisely say of equal opportunity that "there is no support in this conception for the idea of equal government spending per child. . . . [W]hen put in its proper place and weighed against other values, the principle of educational equality appears somewhat less demanding, and some of its apparently implausible implications are muted." That sounds right, but note that Brighouse and Swift are objecting to ineffective and excessively costly policies designed to foster equality. Such policies can lead us to obsess about the equality of inputs. Brighouse and Swift are not rejecting the ideal of educational equality per se. They are taking a realistic perspective on how badly things can go in the policy arena. I respect that.

Adam Swift offers a further thought: it is because education converts into money that money should not convert (unequally) into education.[19] Even if you disagree, you see Swift's point. Swift does not want advantages to be perpetuated and to accumulate across generations. Who can blame him? No one wants to see a reemergence of the kind of hereditary class structure that liberalism overthrew. All of us are on Swift's side here.

That said, let me offer two readings of Swift's point. Are we saying "Because education *captures* money, money should not capture education"? Or are we saying "Because education *creates* capital, capital should not create schools"?

The former is plausible, and presumably is what Swift has in mind. The latter interpretation is highly implausible, and therefore not a charitable interpretation of Swift. The difference: if we are talking about creating wealth, not merely capturing it, then the game is not zero-sum.

NOTES

1. Amartya Sen, personal communication, April 2014.
2. I thank Daniel Weinstock and Debra Satz for helpful ways of putting these concerns.
3. It is impossible to be precise about what it means for children to grow up to be all they can be, but for a social animal, it means roughly this: developing a set of capabilities apt for flourishing within a community, and flourishing in a particular way—namely, by making sure the people around you are better off with you than they would have been without you. In some sense, the bottom line is a psychological fact about social animals: they are better off when people around them *know* that the people around them are better off.
4. Elizabeth Anderson, "Fair Opportunity in Education: A Democratic Equality Perspective," *Ethics* 117 (2007): 595–622, argues that if the justification for fostering a better-educated elite is that creating such an elite is good for everyone, then such an elite must be drawn from all walks of life and must be created within integrated schools, because elites do not learn how to be good for others simply by reading books. They must learn from experience or from the experience of friends what growing up on the wrong side of the tracks is like.
5. Harry Brighouse and Adam Swift, "Putting Educational Equality in Its Place," *Educational Policy and Finance* 3, no. 4 (2008): 444–466, at 446.
6. Brighouse and Swift, "Putting Educational Equality in Its Place," at 448.
7. Harry Brighouse, "Educational Equality and School Reform,"

in Harry Brighouse, Kenneth R. Howe, and James Tooley, ed., *Educational Equality* (New York: Continuum), 30.

8. Brighouse and Swift, "Putting Educational Equality in Its Place," at 447. See also Harry Brighouse and Adam Swift, "Educational Equality Versus Educational Adequacy: A Critique of Anderson and Satz," *Journal of Applied Philosophy* 26, no. 2 (2009): 117–128.

9. I don't mean to say that Brighouse and Swift are committing some inexplicable blunder here. On the contrary, the fact is that virtually none of the people who write about desert are defenders of the concept. But everyday discourse about desert is unintelligible when understood as a justification for departing from equality. Everyday discourse about desert is about something altogether different. The topic is how to respect what bakers do to get the pie to the table. Schmidtz, *The Elements of Justice* (New York: Cambridge University Press, 2006) discusses desert and equality (along with reciprocity and need) as separate elements that constitute justice as a real response to the human condition.

10. Someone who cares about merit does not want to waste inputs, and definitely does not want to waste talent. Realistically, however, wasting potential is inevitable. Every society wastes human capital prodigiously, especially those that officially commit themselves to efficiency rather than to the separateness of individual citizens. When a local concentration of opportunity and imagination comes together in the right way, we see progress. Human progress has no history of being assisted by social engineers. Leaps are always more or less unpredictable strokes of luck, produced by people suddenly finding themselves free to pursue their own vision *at their own expense*. We seem to see more good luck in countries where good luck is celebrated rather than condemned.

11. Adam Swift, *How Not to Be a Hypocrite: School Choice for the Morally Perplexed Parent* (London: Routledge, 2003), 12.

12. Swift, *How Not to Be a Hypocrite*, 14.

13. Swift, *How Not to Be a Hypocrite*, 19–20.

14. Swift, *How Not to Be a Hypocrite*, 20.
15. See also Swift, *How Not to Be a Hypocrite*, x.
16. See Brighouse and Swift, "Putting Equality in Its Place."
17. See Schmidtz, *The Elements of Justice*, for further discussion.
18. Brighouse, *Educational Equality*, 31.
19. Swift, *How Not to Be a Hypocrite*, 12.

4

Justice and the Division of Labor

THEME: TEACHING STUDENTS TO BE COMPLETE citizens is a big job. However, it does not encompass everything. What should schools be able to do for students? What does that have to do with justice? What does that imply about responsibilities of individual teachers?

Plato's theory of justice is not my favorite theory, but it is instructive here. Plato's *Republic* supposed we could learn about justice in an individual soul by looking at justice in the city—he called the latter "justice writ large." Philosophers ever since have been intrigued but skeptical, suspecting that in some ways justice of the soul (that is, doing justice to the parts of one's soul) is unlike justice of the polis (that is, members of a community doing justice to each other).

Justice in our schools (a question of how to do justice to our students) is not like justice in the larger polis, either. If there is a connection, it is something interesting rather than obvious. What academic philosophers say about justice has mostly concerned justice writ large. Hardly any commentary has been specifically about justice in our schools. Thus, when it comes to educational justice, we should consider the possibility that much of our theorizing about justice so far is no more than an analogy.

THEORY AND PRACTICE

On some conceptions, caring about justice contrasts with caring about consequences. To some theorists, this is a license to see justice as possibly contrary to anything we have reason to want on humanitarian grounds. On one hand, part of justice's point is to trump considerations of utility in particular cases. But consider that, somewhat confusingly, there is *value* in being able to count on justice to trump case by case calculations of value. To David Hume, therein lies justice's precise point. *Justice is a set of mutual expectations that enables us to trust each other enough to be better off together than apart.*

Justice makes for a better world by taking case-by-case decisions out of people's hands. That is how justice enables us to live among and deal with other people. For example, hospitals committed to justice work better than hospitals would work if they reserved a right to sacrifice one patient to save five.

In more technical terms, justice has a point just in case global optimization and local optimization are not the same thing. This is how justice makes for a better world despite— indeed because of— the fact that justice trumps case-by-case calculation regarding what makes for a better world.

WHAT WE OWE THE CLIENT: TAKING DIVISION OF LABOR SERIOUSLY

It is not an educational system's job to do everything that a just society would do. Plumbers do justice to their society by being good plumbers. Teachers do justice to society by being good teachers. If the playing field is not level, that may make it somebody's job to level it. But even if leveling the field is *somebody's* job, that is not enough to make it education's job.

Perhaps an educational system's role is to develop talent, period. To be clear, "develop talent" does not refer merely to vocational aptitudes. Part of what I have in mind is developing normal human potentials to learn to appreciate art and nature. Learning to reflect on the human condition likewise is part of it: questions about what people can be, not only what people can get.[1] In any case, we have obligations to parents, employers, taxpayers, and so on, yet our direct obligations as teachers begin and end with students. Could an educational system's job be broader than that? Yes, but *no matter how broad an educational system's job is, it will not be an educational system's place to try to do everything a just society does.*

Likewise, it is not an educational system's place to enhance welfare in all of the ways that a good society enhances welfare. Schools embody, and are inspired by, a vision of what children can become. They are a special, specific response to a possibility of success. Welfare safety nets, by contrast, are a special, specific response to a possibility of failure. They, too, embody a vision of a sort. Society may need responses to both, and it makes sense see best responses to real possibilities of success and failure as complementary. But the point here is that society does not need its *schools* to embody best responses to both.

In fact, we arguably need our schools to work hard to avoid being both. Here is why. Suppose a student tells you she needs help. You feel the pull—because you are human and because helping students is what you are here for. Then she elaborates, telling you she needs an A in your class to have a decent chance of getting into Stanford Law School. Knowing what you do about law school admissions, you think she may be right. But this is a case where a school's certification mission demands a level of integrity that the student is asking you to compromise. You feel a pull. But in this case, giving her what she needs *because she needs it* is out of the question. To give her an A is to certify not that she needed it but that she earned it.

We owe it to our students to award grades on the basis of merit, not need, as best we can. We do not want an A to be an indication of how much a student groveled. On one hand, caring about what students need goes with the territory. But this arguably is one respect in which justice in education—what we owe our students—is not like justice writ large. What we owe students is to preserve the integrity of a certification system that becomes pointless if it loses its integrity. We have a duty to give students what they earn: not less, not more. Regarding the narrower aim of helping students as students, we are not in the proper realm of charity. Giving them grades they have not earned goes beyond what we have any right to give.

How can you tell which students deserve an A? As with most major accomplishments, preparing a student to perform at a high level is a complex cooperative project. Parents help. Other teachers help. Untold multitudes of people contribute indirectly. Yet, none of that matters at assessment time, and schools cannot afford to pretend that it does. We assess performance. We know that assessment is an art, not an exact science, and that giving credit where credit is due requires assessment. Yet we learn to track gradations of quality well enough to make our assessments meaningful, artificial though it can be to represent those gradations in quantitative form.

Of course, grading is not always a matter of arithmetic. Often there is no obvious truth about what grade a student deserves. (Should we sometimes reward effort as such, or always grade strictly according to what a student has achieved?) A grader must decide, not simply discover. But although we recognize that grading an essay is a judgment call, we also recognize that it would be unjust if a grader did not even try to be responsive to (perhaps only to) a student's performance.

To give a seemingly small yet instructive example of what is at stake, consider driver's education. Brighouse reports that driver's education courses are a demonstrable failure in Wisconsin.[2] Accident and mortality rates *rise* where driver's education is a required high school course. Why? Perhaps graduates of such courses do not drive more safely, yet do begin driving at a younger age. I do not know. The unintended consequences of driver's education in Wisconsin are palpably tragic in a way that transcends ideology.

The general point, Brighouse might agree, is that proving that one's heart is in the right place is not good enough. Someone whose heart is in the right place does not knowingly waste other people's money on what does not work. We take driver's education seriously as a goal-directed activity. We find out what works, and we stick with it. We find out what does not work, and we shut it down. We do this because it matters. If we fail, people die unnecessarily at the hands of incompetent drivers.

Needless to say, our specific job as teachers has nothing to do with making drivers equally capable. Instead, we want each driver to be *as capable as possible.*

DIVISION OF LABOR AND INEQUALITY

Persistent inequality can be a threat. Yet it is not necessarily so and is not always so. It is within our power to structure a free society so that such excellence as some drivers, some plumbers, and some surgeons achieve is good for everyone. But the job of making inequalities non-threatening is more a job for society than for educational institutions per se. It is a community's job to constitute itself in such a way as to give us reason to celebrate the advanced learning of the people around us.

It is not the job of teachers or schools to structure society, or to make society per se just. The job of schools is to prepare clients to contribute. Or, to avoid suggesting that we prepare students to be mere means to the ends of others, let's say a school's job is to prepare clients to flourish as contributors. That is pretty much it. We are not missing much if we say teachers and schools are tasked with providing a particular good: namely, education.

In passing, I do not deny that schools can and do serve public health missions. Schools might be the most efficient physical locations for administering vaccines or for providing basic child health services such as tests of vision and hearing. I can imagine schools being a reasonably efficient conduit for delivering various child welfare services. I'm not defending any of those programs so much as simply noting that being a purist about a school's educational mission is compatible with using schools as convenient physical facilities—convenient focal points in a community's geography—for pursuing a social agenda.

WE ARRIVE AS CHILDREN

Jal Mehta says that a functional system of practically universal education presupposes an effective welfare safety net for children.[3] That may be, but the fact remains that the educational system is not itself that safety net, and is no substitute for it, either, any more than plumbers are a substitute for it. As just noted, schools can of course be places where teachers and administrators pay attention to evidence of child abuse or other violent crime. But that is not their defining purpose.

A plumber's job is to fix a customer's plumbing. Plumbers need to determine what customers need. It is not their job to determine what makes customers equal. The same can be said of teachers. Notwithstanding the fact that there comes a time when children need to learn how and when and why to treat each other as equals, teaching is about what children need, not what makes children equal: doing what it takes to educate, not what it takes to equalize.

When we consider real conflicts, we reflect on life and work among people who arrive at different times to a world brimming over with historical baggage. In our world, each of us arrives on the scene to find an economic pie already produced, divided, claimed, and in use by someone else. Philosophers are trained to set this detail aside when theorizing about justice, but it is not a detail. Taking it into account changes everything. It arguably matters as much as, if not more than, anything on which our current theories of justice focus.

We arrive in this world as newborn children. We arrive to a community that does not (yet!) need us, and whether our community someday will be better off with us than without us is not a given—indeed, it is life's greatest challenge. And if we aim to make our mark as teachers, our special role is to help prepare the next generation to handle that same challenge.

We are not the first people who need to learn how to earn a place in a community, and we will not be the last. We aspire to make progress, meaning we want those who follow us to have more than what people today would call an equal share.

OPPORTUNITIES TO LEARN AND OPPORTUNITIES TO EQUALIZE

David Miller once said that if he were to discover that France has a better healthcare system than England's, his egalitarian response would be not to call for a redistribution from France to England but to find out what France is doing better and emulate it. His egalitarianism notwithstanding, Miller sees that the point of doing a particular job is to get that job done. There are few jobs whose purpose is to equalize. Sorting out who should be responsible for getting a job done is not a means to the end of equalizing opportunity. The truth is the other way around. Equalizing opportunity helps us to sort out who can be trusted to get the job done.

Likewise, if incoming Stanford freshmen are already well educated, the solution is not to undo the advantages of incoming Stanford freshmen but to find out what made their prior education better and emulate it so that incoming Arizona freshmen might someday be that good. If we did bring Arizona freshmen up to par with Stanford freshmen, Stanford's graduating class might still end up being superior to Arizona's, because four years at Stanford might be more educational than four years at Arizona. But so what? If Arizona graduates are only in the 95th percentile for world income rather than the 98th, there comes a point where the solution is not to close the gap but to grow up.

What it is like to be left behind? One thing will never change: it will always be a disadvantage to be untalented. Hopefully it always will be a disadvantage to be uneducated, because otherwise what we call education is unspeakably corrupt. But if this is a land of opportunity, then vertical mobility would be an observable reality. Education's enduring advantages would not be confined to an upper class whose ranks are set by inheritance. People from other countries would want to move here, especially if they were poor. Having uneducated parents would be less of a disadvantage than being uneducated oneself. In an extreme case of vertical mobility, it could be typical to be richer than one's grandparents were at a comparable age.

BEYOND EQUALITY

Responding to James Tooley, Brighouse says that even if a fully private system could give all students a decent opportunity to educate themselves to a level apt for their community, such a system would not be just unless decent opportunity was guaranteed.[4] With this I disagree (although my role here is to defend markets in education generally, not a fully private system of education in particular). I do not see justice *in education* as concerned with guaranteeing, as opposed to simply delivering. (If someone says private supermarkets are not guaranteed to offer a quart of milk to customers for the price of five minutes of minimum-wage labor, I would say I don't care, so long as supermarkets don't stop!) Moreover, if we had to guarantee what people currently are guaranteed by virtue of having attended a traditional public school, let us acknowledge that this might not be setting the bar very high. But another point might resonate more with Brighouse, and perhaps Tooley as well—namely, that education's point is to give students a shot at (not a guarantee of) going beyond their parents. That is all a parent could ask.

NOTES

1. I thank Susan Mayer for helpful discussion of this point.
2. Harry Brighouse, *On Education* (London: Routledge, 2006), 56.
3. Jal Mehta, *The Allure of Order* (New York: Oxford University Press, 2013), 250.
4. Harry Brighouse, "What's Wrong with Privatising Schools?," *Journal of the Philosophy of Education Society of Great Britain* 38 (2004): 617–631.

5

What's So Good
About Education?

THEME: HERE WE CONSIDER TWIN CONCERNS. First, when a good is a purely positional good, and thus of no particular social value, markets are likely to oversupply it. Second, if education is instead a public good, and indeed a critically valuable public good, then markets are likely to undersupply it.

POSITIONAL GOODS

It is hard to imagine any controversy over whether education is a good thing. But in a way, there is. Some argue that people who are highly educated have an economic advantage over people who are not, which is to say the uneducated are at a disadvantage, which is to say uneducated people are worse off, which means differential access to educational opportunity raises a question of economic justice, and the uneducated have some basis for claiming compensation from the educated.

The argument's premise is that education is a positional good.[1] A positional good is an item whose value depends on how much of the item one holds compared to what other people hold. Insofar as certification is a positional good, the value of a job applicant having a certain qualification depends on whether rival applicants are more qualified than that. Status is one key example. Insofar as a car is a status symbol, it is a positional good. It signifies higher status than those who own lesser vehicles. Other kinds of positional goods have their utility by virtue of locating people in a chain of command or influence. The rank of captain confers a certain status, but how much captains can do with that status will depend on whether they are interacting with privates or generals.

Other kinds of positional goods are skill sets that are advantageous to players of zero-sum games. The payoff for having a good lawyer in an acrimonious lawsuit can depend on whether the other litigant has a great lawyer. Having a master's degree is a job qualification, but how much weight it carries will depend on whether rival applicants have bachelor's degrees or doctorates. In that sense, education— more accurately, certification—is a positional good.

Education being a positional good suggests a moral problem with letting some students grow up to be too excellent. It implies that we are worse off when the people around us become more highly skilled or more highly certified. In this way, the premise that education is a positional good blurs the distinction between a cooperative society and a competitive race.

As Robert Zemsky, William Massy, and Gregory Wegner say, seemingly without embarrassment, "Critics of higher education, and to some extent higher education itself, have misunderstood the core business of these institutions. Whereas most believe the task of universities and colleges is to supply quality educations at reasonable prices, their real business is to sell competitive advantage at necessarily high prices."[2]

I disagree, but one key point must be conceded: virtually anything useful at all could be useful to a player in a zero-sum game. Any good is potentially a positional good.[3] *Anything that is advantageous has the potential to be an advantage.* When we call education a positional good in the sense that it is better to be educated if playing zero-sum games, we say nothing about education per se. We simply are noting that education is advantageous, and that in zero-sum games, any advantage over other players makes other players worse off.

My disagreement with Zemsky, Massy, and Wegner is specifically this: so far as I can see, although education undeniably can be a positional good, it cannot possibly be purely or even primarily positional. Here is why.

Consider that your education gives you an advantage over your rivals only if prospective employers want someone with your education. Do they? An employer takes an interest in your certification only if he or she considers it a sign that you are bringing something real to the table: real training and real aptitude. To have enduring positional value, a certification must survive inspection as a sign of real value.[4] Therefore, before certification can be a positional good, education must first simply be good. At least, it must appear that way to prospective employers, that is, people whose livelihood depends on seeing past mere appearances.

I said your education gives you an advantage only if prospective employers want someone with your education. I do not deny that it is easy to imagine counterexamples—cases where certification give you an advantage because a prospective employer wants someone with your certification, and where this has little to do with your implied skill set. Suppose you belong to the same alumni club as a prospective employer. Suppose the prospective employer values that bit of information not because he or she values your education but because he or she values opportunities to help fellow alumni.[5]

Where does that leave us? For the sake of argument, suppose a prospective employer is intrigued by your application not because you graduated from the same school but because you too flunked out of the same school, and you too are functionally illiterate. Do we want to say being illiterate is a positional good? No. Speaking this loosely about a remotely conceivable case rather than about actual problems would miss the point of worrying about positional goods. We worry about educational status being a positional good only insofar as we see the conferred advantage as systematic. Graduating is a systematic advantage. Flunking out is not a systematic advantage, and would not become so even if those who flunked got together and formed a club.

So far as I can imagine, any positional advantage of education will be systematic only by virtue of implying a genuine likelihood of being able to do a better job. Therefore, despite easily imagined counterexamples, a general truth remains: without denying that the good of education can and obviously does have positional aspects, education is a systematically positional good only if it is not merely positional.[6] A so-called college degree that one can acquire by sending $25 to a mail-order company will not be systematically advantageous even if we easily can imagine it fooling an utterly inexperienced prospective employer.[7]

Some people try to turn the positional good premise into an argument for equal opportunity. Some try to turn the premise into an argument for redistributing the wealth that educated people produce. However, the premise's actual implication is more radical than that. If we truly saw education as merely a positional good, in the same way legal representation is positional, and if we think the effect of our providing education is like locking six-year-olds into twelve years of litigation, where the only way to win is to make classmates lose, what right would we have to make a living providing it? To distribute this so-called good equally would be to ignore the fundamental issue. Education as a merely positional good would be an arms race, and the fundamental solution would be to *ban* it, not merely to equalize access.

I argued that society is not a race. I would never represent the claim as immune to counterexamples. I simply point to a critical grain of truth about what we are preparing our students to achieve: we hope to send our students into the world not to beat other people's students but to make the world a better place for everyone. We want to put our students in a position to live better lives, but we do not mean better at the expense of their competitors. We mean better not only for them but also for their neighbors, customers, employers, and employees.

The positional-good mindset is supposed to be an improvement on the zero-sum mindset. However, so far as I can see, it is the same mindset: the same premise that getting ahead and being left behind are the currency of success and failure in life.

PUBLIC GOODS

While education is in some respects a positional good, it is also sometimes a public good: a good whose availability benefits a whole community. If you build a private driveway and post No Trespassing signs, then you have created a private good. By contrast, if you build roads for the whole neighborhood with unrestricted access, you have created a public good. When public goods are positive-sum, there is something to lament when they are underproduced.

The complementary concern discussed earlier regarding positional goods has to do with goods that tend to be more or less zero-sum—that is, they are good for one person only insofar as they are bad for someone else, a presumed competitor. In any case, that is how they are understood by critics who lament the proliferation of positional goods, and their point is valid as far as it goes. By contrast, public goods are essentially positive-sum. Therefore, on its face, education cannot be both positional and public. Yet I want to concede that education has characteristics of each. So, which is it? Is education a zero-sum game or not?

On my analysis, the Janus-faced character of education amounts roughly to this: certification has characteristics of a zero-sum positional good. By contrast, depending on circumstances, actual learning can be a positive-sum public good. It contingently is a public good when educated people put their talents into positive-sum games—creating goods and services at prices that benefit their trading partners, and creating benefits that ripple throughout a community.[8] Education is a public good when people compete to be of service.

This is true despite the fact that it does not feel that way at the moment when you learn that you have lost a competition to one of your rival job applicants. In that dark moment, the competition feels zero-sum indeed. Nevertheless, the public, including every rival who ever came in second as a job candidate (and who among us has not?), is better off in virtue of jobs in general being held by people who are more rather than less well trained for those positions.

If any of us could push a button to make every one of our fellow citizens better at what they do—better doctors, better plumbers, better teachers—we should push it, even if only out of self-interest. Other things equal, pushing that button moves us into a world where we do better even if we do not respond by raising our own game to the next level. You are not, for example, competing with your surgeon. You *want* your surgeon to be a far better surgeon than you are.

I called education a public good. More precisely, education has the potential to be a public good. A well-ordered society makes it true that education is a public good, serving the interests of future employers, employees, customers, and so on. And making it true that education is a public good is a major achievement on the part of society. To the extent that neighbors who are getting educated are acquiring valuable capacities to help make the world a better place for all of us, the more the better, and we should simply cheer them on.

The Public Good Begins at Home; Our Client Is the Student

I will elaborate, but first, a caveat. As Harry Brighouse rightly stresses, our attitude should be that we work for the student, not for a student's future employer. If we think we need to respond to the needs of future employers, we are exaggerating both education's public aspect and its positional aspect. Our client is the student. To our own employers we have a duty to fulfill the terms of our contract, but it is to students alone that we have a sacred duty to find the absolute best within us and bring it to class.

Without meaning to retreat from this point, let me present a qualification. I teach high school teachers right now. When I do, all of us understand that my students (the high school teachers) are not the point of the exercise. Our ultimate point revolves not around my students but around my students' students. Perhaps this is not exactly a counterexample, but it is something to keep in mind. To acknowledge that our students are teachers themselves is to acknowledge the service they provide to students of their own. Thus, not every instance of seeing my students as means to the ends of others is morally problematic. To prepare our students to be of service is to treat them as both means and ends, so long as being of service in that particular way is their idea.

Harry says our client is our student, not the student's future employer. I agree. I would add that our client typically is not any of the people our student could end up serving. We are not training students to be mere means. We think the best life a person could live does in fact involve being a great neighbor, great friend, great partner, and so on. We all should aspire to thrive in such a way that the world is better off with us than without us. Yet, we are not community property. Neither are our students. We aspire to put our students in a position to contribute, not to sacrifice. We teach them to contribute because making a contribution is part of what make a life worth living.

The Point Is What Our Students Can Be, Not Only What They Can Do

Accordingly, we need to make some budgeting decisions at the big-picture level, where we think about what makes it right that we lived: what enriches and redeems life, not only what extends it. As Harry Brighouse says, we all need income, and most of us need to know that we did something to earn our income. But that tells us something about education's intrinsic value, too, not only its instrumental value. The best we could do to honor and encourage our future Mozarts and Shakespeares is not to subsidize them but to prepare their customer base to relish the challenge of knowing excellence when they hear it. As Brighouse's says, we "need not just income but a sense of self-reliance."[9] This is as true of great artists as of anyone else.[10]

CONCLUSION

What would I do to ensure that education is a public rather than positional good? I would first say that answering this question is a task for a whole society rather than for an educational system in particular. The job of a whole society is to be a place where it is good to have neighbors, and even better to have educated neighbors. We care that everyone receives as excellent an opportunity to get an education as we can possibly provide, but that is because education is good, and because more is better, especially for those who otherwise would have less. It is not because there is some premium on making sure that everyone has the same.

To the extent that it is better to have educated neighbors, education is more or less a public good. It is not a zero-sum game. It may be positional in a particular context, but it is not merely positional. If there are times and places where that cannot be taken for granted, then that is one problem. In the societies we know, however, it surely can be taken for granted. In that case, the problem becomes one of ensuring that there is sufficient demand to drive people to become the kind of educated person that other people would want as a plumber, doctor, or other supplier of the services that make communities the loci of human flourishing that they are.

If I could push a button to get the government entirely out of the business of funding education, I would not push it. Separately, if I could push a button today that would get the government entirely out of the business of directly delivering educational services, I would not push it. However, I certainly would ask, "When if ever do we have sufficient reason to believe that government needs to deliver educational services in a way that repudiates a parent's right to say no and walk away?"

There is an alternative. It would be an experiment, and to some people it would be scary in the way that experiments tend to be scary. If the government could simply enter the market with a competitive product, as the post office began to do some years ago, the quality of service might go up, as did quality in postal services. In some respects, our system of education is better, and more effective, than the business model of the post office of my youth.

Interestingly, however, the business model of our current system of education may not be as good as the business model of our current post office. The way education is provided today is like paying for postage with a property tax rather than having customers pay postage for each service, deciding case by case whether the service is worth the cost. If we handled the mail as if postage had to be paid for by property taxes, the service would be rotten. In that hypothetical case, if we could not imagine any other way to do it, and doubted that we had a better alternative, we would be wrong.

So, despite none of us having any clue about what an ideal post office would be like, we are in a position to identify meaningful improvements on the post office of my youth. We can say with confidence that allowing private competition was useful in spurring the post office to pay more attention to whether customers were being well served.

We also can say that while the post office lost its legal battle for a monopoly in the service of delivering parcels, the post office won its battle to retain its monopoly in the cheap delivery of first-class mail. The post office's argument (as I recall the Canadian debate) was that delivery of local downtown business mail was profitable, but the post office needed those profits in order to be able to subsidize the delivery of rural mail. While a private company such as UPS or FedEx might be far better than the post office at delivering local downtown business mail, it might neglect even to try to deliver rural mail; meanwhile, the post office would no longer have the revenue to subsidize its rural service. That argument, as I recall, won the day. Whether that is a strong argument depends on the facts, but it is not easily dismissed, even granting the premise that private companies would provide superior service in the most lucrative markets.

Does any of that apply to arguments about the privatization of schools, or more conservatively to simply allowing private competition? Or suppose, even more conservatively, that we are talking about allowing a degree of competition within the public sector—that is, charter schools. Could we imagine such a thing as "charter" letter carriers? Perhaps charter letter carriers could officially work for the post office but be paid on commission rather than on salary. Or charter carriers could contract with particular senders to handle their mail, or with particular addressees to deliver their mail. You could imagine letting cities experiment, and you could imagine cities learning important lessons from their own and each other's experiments. They might not all draw the same lesson. Presumably they would not need to all draw the same lesson at the same time. When independent decision makers draw different lessons, over time society is learning.

NOTES

1. See also Harry Brighouse and Adam Swift, "Equality, Priority, and Positional Goods," *Ethics* 116 (2006): 471–497. For a response to Brighouse and Swift, see Christopher Freiman, "Priority and Position," *Philosophical Studies* 167 (2014): 341–360.
2. Robert Zemsky, William Massy, and Gregory Wegner, *Remaking the American University: Market-Smart and Mission-Centered* (New Brunswick, NJ: Rutgers University Press, 2005), 71.
3. I thank Bas van der Vossen for the observation.
4. We can of course imagine counterexamples. If an employer is legally required to hire only people with Stanford degrees, or

only people with a union card or a green card, then of course an employer could be keen to see such certification without thinking it indicates anything positive about the candidate.

5. I thank Keith Hankins for the thought.

6. Brighouse and Swift correctly say it is more accurate to describe education as having positional aspects than to describe education as a positional good. "Equality, Priority, and Positional Goods," 472.

7. Perhaps this is a not terribly unrealistic worry. Suppose an expensive education is a signal of something important, but not by virtue of learning at the expensive school being especially excellent. Rather, the amount that a student pays in tuition is strongly correlated with how much attention parents paid to raising that student to be a lifelong learner. Applicants whose parents care enough to spend a fortune on education therefore turn out to be systematically better— not because their education per se was systematically better but because in general they were raised by parents who paid more attention to them.

8. Alan Berube of the Brookings Institution reports that workers who lack a high school diploma have been more likely to keep their jobs in the current recession if they live in areas with the highest concentrations of people with college degrees. For example, "if you're a worker without a high school diploma, you are better off being in a highly educated labor market like Seattle than being in a less educated labor market like Scranton." Quoted in Sara Murray, "Close Does Count When It Comes to Jobs, Education," *Wall Street Journal*, November 8, 2010.

9. Harry Brighouse, *On Education* (London: Routledge, 2006), 29.

10. Brighouse adds that a sense of self-reliance is socially constructed but no less real for that (*On Education*, 33). To be self-reliant in a community is not to be a hermit but to be a trading partner—someone who acquires some goods by producing them, and acquires other goods by producing goods for trade.

PART II

DEBATING MARKETS
IN EDUCATION

HARRY BRIGHOUSE

THE AIMS FOR A SYSTEM

First we have to define what we want to achieve. Most wealthy developed countries have elites whose children, on average, seem, from the evidence, to get a pretty good academic education. They produce at least some highly skilled mathematicians, writers, computer scientists, communicators, entrepreneurs, and scientists. These people have been educated well, at least in traditional academic terms, by some combination of teachers, parents, peers, and other members of their community.

But the proportion of the population that achieves at that high academic level seems to vary among countries. And in some countries—notably the United States and the United Kingdom—substantial proportions of the overall population emerge into adulthood lacking the kind of academic skills that are highly valued in labor markets and that seem to be essential for successfully navigating the complexities of life in a capitalist society. And although the largest proportion of the population, which is neither bound for the elite nor condemned to precariousness, possesses academic skills that would be the envy of their great-great-grandparents, complaints that schools are highly inefficient and waste opportunities to develop human capital abound. In 2014–15 in the United States, despite an increase in the graduation rate, only 83 percent of students graduated from high school. That percentage includes those who acquire alternative credentials, some of which are of questionable value, and it also varies considerably between states: Nevada, the District of Columbia, Oregon, and New Mexico all had graduation rates of below 75 percent. Furthermore, despite a several-year increase in graduation rates, scores on college admissions tests (the ACT and SAT) were flat, and scores on the National Assessment of Educational Progress, which researchers regard as the most reliable gauge of educational performance, were down. High school graduation prospects in the United States, like gauges of educational success everywhere, correlate closely with socioeconomic status. Whereas overall 83 percent of students graduated in 2014–15, only 74.6 percent of African American students and only 76 percent of low-income students graduated. College matriculation rates similarly reflect class background, as does attendance at elite colleges. Among those who attend college, students from lower-income backgrounds are substantially less likely to graduate than those from more affluent backgrounds. There's a consensus that lower-income children in many wealthy countries are not achieving at the rate they could.

I'm going to take it for granted that, for any society, it is desirable, other things equal, to raise the mean level of educational accomplishment, and that whatever the mean level of educational accomplishment, it would be better for it to be achieved more cost-effectively than at present. It is better that people are better educated, because for any given person the better educated she is, the better equipped she is to accomplish what she wants to with her life, and the better equipped she is to contribute to meeting the needs and interests of other people. It is better that education is provided more cost-effectively because efficiency is good; it frees up more resources to be spent in other valuable ways. I shall also take for granted that education is currently delivered less cost-effectively, at least in some countries—my main foci will be the United States and the United Kingdom, for the simple reason that I know a good deal about their schooling systems—than it could feasibly be. So one goal should be to make educational provision more efficient.

I'm not going to take it for granted, but am going to argue in Chapter 2, that another urgent goal should be to raise the educational level of the least well-educated 30–40 percent of the population, and that the worse someone's educational prospects, the more urgent it is to raise that person's level of education. In fact, as I'll explain, I believe that several principles should play a role in our decisions about how to structure the education system. Some of these principles concern the content of the kinds of educational goods—the knowledge, skills, attitudes, and dispositions—that students should acquire. In particular, I shall argue that children should develop the knowledge, skills, attitudes, and dispositions that will enable them to be effective contributors to the economy, to be competent democratic citizens, to be able to make their own authentic judgements about how to live their lives, and to have fulfilling personal lives. Other principles concern how these educational goods should be distributed: I'm going to argue that in the contemporary conditions of reasonably wealthy liberal democracies with economic systems in which labor markets play a large role in the allocation of jobs and in which educational achievement and attainment play a substantial role in determining labor market success, focusing on lower achievers, within limits, is a matter of considerable urgency—much greater urgency than, for example, trying to equalize achievement.

This book debates markets in education. What do the principles I suggest we should attend to tell us about the role markets should play in the delivery of schooling in contemporary societies?

My answer to this question is distributed over three chapters. In Chapter 3 I identify markets that currently frame the provision of schooling—focusing especially on the labor market for teachers, which affects how teaching talent gets developed, and on the housing market, which, in combination with the labor market and government decisions, affects which students get taught by which teachers. As things stand, and without governmental measures designed to counteract their effects, these markets already, if stealthily, inhibit our ability to reach the goals we should set for ourselves. I do not call for these markets to be eliminated. Neither does almost anyone else. Most people accept that markets of these kinds play an ineliminable role in education. So I cheerfully concede in Chapter 3 that no market-free approach to education policy is available.

Chapter 4 explores the central current proposals for extending the role of markets in the provision of schooling, which fall under the very broad rubric of "school choice." School choice proposals come in many different forms. In several countries all (publicly supported) schools are, in some sense, schools of choice: in most parts of England, for example, parents have to register several choices among primary and secondary schools, and those preferences play some role in determining which school their child attends. But even in countries such as the United States, where the norm is that children attend their neighborhood school, alternative systems have developed. The most notable are charter schools and voucher schools. Charter schools are funded by the government, usually under a different and looser regulatory system than the traditional schools with which they compete, and are usually run by nongovernmental organizations (normally nonprofits, but in some cases profit-making companies). All children within some jurisdiction are eligible to attend a given charter school, and parents can opt in; if a school is oversubscribed, its intake is determined by a lottery. Voucher schools represent a more radical privatization of schooling: they are run by private organizations (again, usually, not-for-profit), and eligible students are funded by a voucher—a per-child subvention provided by the local or state government. Voucher systems vary considerably in which children are counted as eligible: the first voucher system in the United States, in Milwaukee, Wisconsin, determines eligibility by reference to the official poverty line and requires oversubscribed schools to use lotteries, but Florida, for example, allows any child who has been attending a public school deemed to be failing over a certain period to take a voucher, and

Cleveland, Ohio, allows voucher schools limited discretion over which children attend.

Chapter 4 comes in two parts. First, I provide a theoretical case that opening schooling fully to markets would be incompatible with the goals I argued for in Chapter 2, partly because of the behavior we should expect from families, and partly because markets in schooling are highly imperfect. Of course, even if my case is watertight, it could still be that extending markets in schooling would *improve* the system's achievement of those goals. So the second part of Chapter 4 reviews some of the evidence we have about the effects of various market reforms—in particular, voucher and charter schools in the United States, about which we have a great deal of evidence—and demonstrates that, in fact, these reforms have not had substantial benefits. The evidence does not suggest that the market reforms that have been tried are disastrous for the goals I set out, but neither does it suggest that they further those goals.

Chapter 4 will disappoint some readers. I do not argue that charter schools and voucher schools should be abolished, or even that they inevitably conflict with the principles to which we should hold ourselves. In fact, I think that charter schools could have a valuable, if limited, role to play in improving schooling. I was even for a long time an unenthusiastic defender of the voucher program in Milwaukee, until the regulations were changed to take the focus off low-income children, and even now I am ambivalent. But what I shall argue in Chapter 4 is that markets are, for the most part, a distraction. The burden of Chapter 4 will be to persuade the reader that markets should not be the driving principle of changes in education policy.

I said that markets are a distraction. But a distraction from what? Many opponents of choice say things like "We shouldn't be introducing voucher schools, or charter schools, or free schools [roughly the British equivalent of charter schools]; instead we should be making sure that regular public schools are all good [or, if the opponent is very ambitious, *great*] schools." But how do we ensure that regular public schools are as good as they could be (however good that is)? Many supporters of school choice are well-intentioned and honest supporters of good schooling who have despaired of efforts to improve traditional public schools. Improving schools systematically is extremely difficult, and the track record isn't very good. Even if we knew some way of doing it in a systematic and far-reaching way, explaining how to do it would surely take more space than we have in this book, and would be some way beyond my expertise. But no very clear way of doing it is known! In Chapter 5 I'll offer some brief comments suggesting alternative measures aimed at making schooling more efficient and improving schooling for less advantaged students.

First, though, in Chapter 1, I shall say something, especially for the reader who is not familiar with the way political philosophers think, about the kind of theorizing this essay represents.

1

Setting the Stage

MORAL AND POLITICAL PHILOSOPHERS DISTINGUISH two different kinds of theorizing about values and principles: ideal theorizing and non-ideal theorizing. The end goal of this essay is not, for me, a description of what the education system would look like in an ideal society. Even if I knew with more confidence than I do exactly what principles of justice should guide the design of an ideally just society, I would hesitate in trying to describe the structure of the education system that society should adopt. Instead I want to contribute to a discussion about what the educational system should be like in societies that fall short of being just in particular ways—specifically, in the ways in which the societies that my readers inhabit fall short of being just.

The essay is, in other words, an exercise in non-ideal theorizing—figuring out what principles we should act on, and what we should do, in a society that falls short of justice and will not, as a result of our best feasible actions, become just. But non-ideal theorizing typically also deploys and rests on ideal theorizing in some way. So it is worth spending a little time explaining the two types of theorizing and how they are related. It is helpful to start with the question of why we do moral theory itself. We want moral theories for three main purposes. The first is descriptive.

We want, simply, to know what values matter and how much they matter relative to one another. Is courage valuable? Is modesty? Does equality matter, and if so, under what interpretation? Does freedom matter? If equality and freedom both matter, which matters more, and by how much? The second purpose of moral theory is evaluative. We care about the state of the world; we want to know how good it is and in which ways it is good, and how bad it is and in which ways it is bad. The third purpose is to guide our practical reason. We want to know what we are permitted to do, and what we are obliged to do, in the circumstances in which we find ourselves, and moral theory is an indispensable means to doing that.

Ideal theory—or a theory of ideals—is just whatever is involved in fulfilling that first, descriptive purpose. Using whatever means are available, the moral theorist attempts, with as much precision as possible and at as high a level of abstraction as possible, to identify values—courage, equality, relief of suffering, freedom, and so on—and to work out how important they are relative to one another. While most moral theorists would not describe themselves as Platonists, the Platonic picture is helpful: we can think of values as really existing in a formal realm, and the descriptive task as tentatively mapping that realm, using intuition, reflection, thought experiments, logic, and the other usual methods of philosophy. Ideal theory, on this understanding, is a theory of ideal values.

Ideal theory is essential for the second purpose of moral theory. We want to evaluate the state of the world, and in doing so we deploy the moral categories that we have identified in ideal theory. If, for example, we have identified some variant of a principle of equality of resources as an important value, we deploy that when scrutinizing the evidence about inequality of income and wealth within and between countries to evaluate how equal or unequal the world we inhabit is and thus how good or bad it is with respect to the value of equality.[1] This allows us to know the extent to which the world is non-ideal in this respect.

So what is non-ideal theorizing? The third purpose of moral theory is to guide our practical reason: it helps us work out what we should do in the world. And in a world such as ours, which is in various ways imperfect, and which we expect to remain imperfect in at least some of those ways no matter what we do, we should not necessarily act in exactly the ways we would act if we were in a just or ideal world. Non-ideal theorizing is what we do when we think about what principles should guide actions within circumstances that are, in whatever ways, not ideal. In other words, it fulfills the third purpose of moral theory that I've identified, but in non-ideal circumstances.

Non-ideal theorizing requires us to specify the circumstances for which we are doing the theorizing, because there are many different kinds of non-ideal circumstances. For example, Francis Schrag elegantly argues that the kind of traits that educators would be obliged to foster in Jewish students living in Berlin in the 1930s might be quite different from the traits they would be obliged to foster in children in a democratic and broadly liberal (even though unjust) polity such as the contemporary United States. Schrag's immediate interest is in Nazi Germany; ours here is, as I have said, in the way the education system should be structured in the societies my readers inhabit.[2]

One complication arising from this ambition is that even modern liberal democratic societies are non-ideal in different ways. Norway is happier and less unequal than the United States; Germany is less unequal and has a more robust welfare state than the United States, but is more unequal and has a less robust welfare state than Sweden. If we define poverty as living in a household that has less than half of the median household income, UNICEF reports that Norway has a child poverty rate of 3.4 percent, the Netherlands 9.8 percent, the United Kingdom 15.4 percent, and the United States 21.9 percent. If we adjust the definition to 40 percent or less of the median household income, the UK rate falls to 5.5 percent but the US rate only falls to 14.1 percent.[3] Every Briton—like the vast majority of non-Britons living in the United Kingdom—enjoys access to reasonably high-quality primary healthcare, more or less free at the point of delivery. In 2010, 18.2 percent of Americans, and 10 percent of American children, lacked health insurance coverage of any kind, meaning that, in practice, only emergency care was readily available to them. By 2016, due to passage of the Affordable Care Act, these figures had fallen to 10 percent and 5 percent, respectively (though rates differed considerably among states, and many of the insured pay considerable out-of-pocket expenses for primary care). The point here is not that a particular country is more or less just than another, but that one country is very probably not exactly as just or unjust as another, some are unjust in different ways, and the social and economic context within which the education system is nested varies considerably even among wealthy liberal democracies.

An additional complication is that these countries have substantially different education systems, which yield, according to international comparisons, substantially different educational outcomes. The United Kingdom, Australia, and New Zealand all have highly elaborate school choice systems *within* the public sector. The United Kingdom allows schools a limited amount of discretion in selecting students, including on the basis of their academic promise. The United States largely eschews academic selection and mainly deploys neighborhood-based schooling, with choice systems operating at the margins (except in a few cities and some states). Germany uses academic selection early, and pretty much across the board. France and Singapore have highly prescriptive national curriculums, whereas many US states have only limited state standards that are very lightly enforced. In the Netherlands the vast majority of students attend privately run schools that are funded through a progressive per-student funding system. In the United Kingdom schools with high concentrations of disadvantaged students attract much higher funding than other schools, whereas in the United States the localized system of funding means that children in areas with high real estate values attend schools much better funded than schools in areas with lower real estate values.

Measured outcomes also vary among and within countries. According to the 2015 Programme for International Student Assessment (PISA) tests carried out by the OECD, the average achievement in mathematics in the Netherlands, Denmark, and Finland is significantly higher than in New Zealand and the United Kingdom, where in turn it is significantly higher than in the United States. With respect to science, achievement in Finland is significantly higher than in the United Kingdom, Germany, and the Netherlands, which in turn have higher achievement than in Norway and the United States. The story with reading is that Finland outstrips Germany and the Netherlands, which in turn outperform the United Kingdom and the United States.

Within countries, too, outcomes vary both by region and by demography. In the United Kingdom a 2007 study showed that only 53.5 percent of eleven-year-olds eligible for free school meals reached expectations for their grade level, compared with 75.5 percent of the overall population. Another study showed that half of white British boys eligible for free school meals had results in the bottom quartile of the distribution at age sixteen. Only 19 percent of white British boys eligible for free school meals achieved five or more grades of C or above on GCSEs (national exams taken at age sixteen), 31.7 percentage points below the figure for all sixteen-year-olds.[4] In the United States, while the test score gap between blacks and whites has narrowed steadily (with a plateau in the 1990s) since the 1954 Supreme Court decision *Brown v. Board of Education*, which outlawed "separate but equal" education, the gap in achievement (whether it is measured in test scores, high school graduation, or years of schooling) between more affluent and less affluent students has steadily widened since the 1970s.[5]

Throughout my part of the book the real-world examples will mostly be drawn from school systems in the United Kingdom and the United States. This reflects the fact that these are the countries whose school systems I know well. It is also convenient, though, because the United Kingdom and the United States have nicely contrasting schooling systems with respect to choice and other features. But it will help to fix ideas if I specify more widely applying conditions that constitute the background against which the education systems about which I am theorizing operate. Some of these parameters are, in my opinion (though I shall not argue for this), non-ideal—that is, they constitute injustices. Others are not, or at least might not be, non-ideal. The reader need not always agree with my assessment; just recognize that I might offer different theoretical and practical considerations if the parameters were different.

First, I assume that the education system is nested in a broadly democratic polity. The government is accountable to the people through regular elections in which most of the population can vote and in which significant majorities can usually block policies that they strongly oppose. Second, I assume capitalist economies with reasonably well-functioning housing markets and labor markets. (The stricture about labor markets is particularly significant: if the government could conscript labor into teaching, that could significantly reduce the costs of providing education, and if it could direct teachers to teach in schools with high concentrations of disadvantaged students, that would reduce the public costs of benefiting less advantaged students.) Along with assuming that the economy is capitalist, I assume not entirely predictable fluctuations in employment levels and in economic growth. I also assume that there are considerable limits on how much redistribution from high-income to low-income citizens the government can, in practice, effect. Of course, wealthy capitalist democracies vary considerably in how much redistribution they engage in: both the United States and the United Kingdom are much more unequal than, and have considerably lower social mobility than, Sweden or Denmark. I do not assume of any society that it *cannot* do more redistribution than it does, but I do assume that it *will not* do *much* more redistribution than it does. Thus I make my final assumption, which is that child poverty rates will not change a great deal. In the United Kingdom child poverty rates did, in fact, decline considerably in the 2000s, and it is clear that willing governments can use tax and employment policy to alter child poverty rates. But I do not see great political will to do so, at least in the English-speaking world.

NOTES

1. Ronald Dworkin, "What Is Equality? Part 2: Equality of Resources," *Philosophy and Public Affairs* 10, no. 4 (1981): 283–345.
2. Francis Schrag, "Moral Education in the 'Badlands,'" *Journal of Curriculum Studies* 42, no. 2 (2010): 149–163.
3. Note that economic crises can give rise to sudden drops in the median income, which artificially lowers the poverty rate defined in relative terms. My point here is just that there is considerable variation, and that variation might matter for practical and even theoretical purposes.
4. Members of other racial and ethnic groups eligible for free school meals outperform white British boys, but within each group social class standing affects outcomes in a similar way as for whites.
5. Sean F. Reardon, "The Widening Academic Achievement Gap Between the Rich and the Poor: New Evidence and Possible Explanations," in *Whither Opportunity? Rising Inequality, Schools, and Children's Life Chances*, ed. Greg J. Duncan and Richard J. Murnane (New York: Russell Sage Foundation, 2011), 91–116.

2

What Should Schooling Be About and How Should It Be Distributed?

THE QUESTION WE ARE ADDRESSING is what role markets should play in the delivery of schooling in wealthy democracies. Enthusiasts for, and opponents of, markets can sometimes sound as if they think this question is itself a value question. But it is not. It's a mistake to take a "principled stand" for, or against, markets in education. Instead we work out what the goals of the education system should be, and we ask what institutions are most likely to achieve those goals. So in this chapter, drawing on the account I have developed with my colleagues Helen Ladd, Susanna Loeb, and Adam Swift in our book *Educational Goods*, I shall lay out, and partially defend, an account of the goals we should have for an education system.[1]

It makes sense to distinguish two kinds of goals one could have for an education system. The first concerns educational achievement: what knowledge, skills, dispositions, and attitudes should children learn? The second concerns the distribution of that achievement: what kinds of inequality of achievement are acceptable or even desirable?

WHAT KIND OF ACHIEVEMENT?

In this section I'll suggest that education should aim to develop in children the knowledge, skills, attitudes, and dispositions that would be needed for five capabilities: economic productivity, personal autonomy, democratic competence, healthy personal relationships, and personal fulfilment.

The case for *economic productivity* is fairly simple. In market economies, unless they have extremely wealthy parents or some other source of guaranteed income, people's flourishing depends on their ability to participate effectively in the economy, simply because everyone needs an income. Their flourishing also depends on others contributing effectively to the economy: the increased economic capability of the educated person increases the aggregate stock of human capital that society can harness to the benefit of all. Exactly what it takes to equip people to become economically productive, of course, depends both on specifics about the way the economy works and on how broadly we understand economic productivity. To illustrate the first point: skills that are extremely productive in some stages of technological development can become economically valueless fairly quickly, such as the physical setting of metal type for printed materials. In general, we seem to be living through a period in which many tasks that once required complex human skills are rapidly being mechanized, so those specific skills are no longer economically useful. To illustrate the second point: while it is important for individuals to be able to earn an income in whatever labor markets they actually confront, many contributions to the economy may not, for various reasons, yield rewards that reflect the extent of their contribution, yet we would want to consider them as part of the economy nevertheless.

Personal autonomy is valuable because we benefit from the ability to make and act on well-informed and well-thought-out judgments about both how to live and what to do in our everyday lives. For human beings to flourish they need to engage in activities and relationships that reflect their sense of who they are and what matters to them. Some people may flourish within the constraints laid down by the religious strictures of their parents, but others may be stunted by those same requirements. Parents—and educators—cannot know in advance which children will fit into which category. Knowledge of other religious views, and of non-religious views, supports flourishing by giving the individual the opportunity to choose alternatives, or aspects of them.[2] Even with knowledge of the alternatives, the self-knowledge, habits of mind, and strength of character to make the appropriate alternative choice are also needed. The same logic applies to choice of occupation. Some children find themselves under very heavy parental pressure to pursue a particular occupational path: possessing sufficient knowledge of the relevant variables, and sufficient self-knowledge and fortitude, enables them to make the parental pressure an appropriate influence on their choice. Whether ultimately they choose for or against will depend on their own, independent judgment of the fit between the occupation and their interests. Autonomy doesn't only matter for major life decisions: in their everyday lives, people make and act on judgments about what to do that are not fully determined by their most fundamental commitments, such as what to eat, what leisure activities to engage in, whom to talk to and about what. These choices, too, will typically contribute more to their flourishing if they have a reasonable range of valuable options and the capacity to make, and act on, their own judgments.

Now let's turn to *democratic competence*. In democratic societies, when someone votes, that person is normally calling on the government to use its unique coercive powers to impose its will on others. People benefit from the ability to use their political institutions to press their own interests, and they benefit from others being able and inclined to give due weight to *their* legitimate interests. So it is valuable to instill in children the personal attributes that enable and incline them to eventually become effective and morally decent participants in social life and political processes. The knowledge and skills needed for democratic competence are various, and depend on context. A basic understanding of the history and structures of a society's political institutions is usually valuable, as is a basic ability and disposition to bring reason and evidence to bear on claims and arguments made by others. Institutions vary considerably in the informational demands they place on citizens and in the deliberative resources they provide. The US electoral system, for example, with its numerous levels of government and frequent elections, places high demands on citizens, especially in those states where candidates for most elections may not register their party affiliation on the ballot paper. Political advertising gives citizens very limited help in their deliberations. Democratic systems with fewer and less frequent elections and more controls over political advertising may make it easier for citizens to participate in an informed and meaningful way, and thus will require less in terms of knowledge, skills, dispositions, and attitudes. Many policy issues are hard for citizens to evaluate because they lack a good understanding of the way the institutions work and of the possible side effects of any proposed reform. Theorists disagree about exactly what constitutes democratically competent behavior. For some theorists obedience to the law suffices; for others actual engagement in the political process is required; yet others hold that competent behavior might sometimes involve challenging or breaking the law even in a democracy. Exactly what the capability for democratic competence requires depends on settling these issues. But on any account, *being able to* engage is required, and acquiring the capacity for democratic competence is important.[3]

Recent empirical literature confirms the commonsense view that *successful personal relationships* are at the center of a happy life. The same is probably true of a flourishing life. For most of us, flourishing requires a variety of relationships, including lasting and intimate relationships with others. People derive meaning from their relationships with their spouses, parents, children, and close friends, and even from looser ties with acquaintances in their neighborhoods and at work. Successful personal relationships require certain attributes—emotional openness, kindness, a willingness to take risks with one's feelings, trust—that do not develop automatically but are in large part responses to one's environment. We can hope that families will provide the kind of environment in which children will develop these qualities, but not all will, and even if they do, this process can be supplemented and reinforced by other institutions, including schools.

Healthy personal relationships are important, but so are complex and satisfying labor and projects that engage one's physical, aesthetic, intellectual, and spiritual faculties. Schools are particularly well positioned to create the knowledge, skills, attitudes, and dispositions that enable *personal fulfilment*. People find great satisfaction in music, literature, and the arts; games and sports; mathematics and science; and religious practice. In these and other activities, they exercise and develop their talents, and meet complex challenges. Throughout history a great deal of paid work has been dreary and/or carried out in the context of stressful status hierarchies, and this will continue to be the case in the foreseeable future. People in such jobs have limited opportunities to flourish at work. School is a place in which children's horizons can be broadened. They can be exposed to—and can develop enthusiasms for and competence in—activities that they never would have encountered through familial and communal networks, and which sometimes suit them better than any they would have encountered in those ways. The capacity to find joy and fulfillment from experiences and activities is at the heart of a flourishing life.[4]

DISTRIBUTION: EQUALITY AND PRIORITIZING THE LESS ADVANTAGED

Now let's think about how educational outcomes should be distributed. It's commonplace for politicians and educational leaders to talk about "equity" in education when they are concerned with how to distribute educational resources and with supporting programs targeting less advantaged students. But Christopher Jencks once commented that "the enduring popularity of equal educational opportunity probably derives from the fact that we can all define it in different ways without realizing how profound our differences really are,"[5] and I strongly suspect that the same could now be said of equity. Can we get more precise about how educational resources should be distributed?

I think we can, by looking at the fundamental values that should animate us when it comes to distribution. I'm going to explore two principles. The first is equality: the idea that the valuable educational outcomes I've outlined in the preceding section should be equally distributed. The second is prioritizing the less advantaged: the idea that valuable educational outcomes should be distributed in a way that, overall, makes better the lives of those whose lives go worse.

Let's start with equality. The fundamental reason for caring about educational equality is closely related to the reason for caring about equality of opportunity in general. Modern industrial societies are structured so that socially produced rewards—income, wealth, status, and positions in the occupational structure, along with the opportunities for self-exploration and fulfilment that come with these things—are distributed unequally. Educational achievement is a crucial mechanism for gaining access to these rewards; a person's level and kind of educational achievement typically have a major influence on where she will end up in the distribution of those potentially life-enhancing goods. The thought is just that it is unfair if some get a worse education than others, because, through no fault of their own, this puts them at a disadvantage in the competition for these unequally distributed, and valuable, goods.

So the intuitive case for educational equality is fairness-based; more specifically, it depends on the idea that, in order to be legitimate, inequalities of outcome should result from fair procedures, and fair procedures are those in which various characteristics of a person are prevented from influencing that person's prospects. The idea is invoked by people who think, for example, that it is wrong for racial characteristics to influence outcomes, and therefore seek to ensure that education for racial minorities is as good as education for whites; or who think that gender should not influence outcomes, and so demand that boys and girls should have equally good education.

One source of unequal influence over prospects that is widely regarded as unfair is social class. Think of the call in the United States to eliminate the achievement gap. If understood strictly, this demands that there should be no difference in achievement between children born into lower or higher socioeconomic classes. In the United Kingdom, which has an education system quite different from that in the United States but is similar in having a high degree of economic inequality relative to other wealthy democracies, successive secretaries of state for education have called more explicitly for the elimination of any influence of social class on educational achievement.[6] They adopt what Christopher Jencks calls a "weak humane justice" conception of educational equality: an individual's prospects for educational achievement may be a function of that individual's talent and effort, but they should not be influenced by her social class background.[7]

In an unequal society this conception of educational equality is very demanding. Given what we know about the influence of social class on achievement, for example, it seems to require that very considerably more resources be spent on educating children from lower socioeconomic backgrounds than on children from more advantaged backgrounds, and that these resources be spent effectively. It also strongly suggests that measures going beyond the education system should be adopted. If it is not known how to educate large numbers of children who are raised in relative poverty to the levels that can be achieved by more advantaged children in the same society, for example, the principle demands the elimination of child poverty.[8]

Standing alone, however, this conception permits (although it does not require) considerable inequality of both educational resources and educational achievement, as long as those inequalities do not track social class. For example, it is consistent with concentrating resources on those who have high levels of talent and motivation, with the aim of producing very high levels of achievement for them, while leaving those with lower levels of talent and motivation to fend for themselves, with, presumably, very low levels of achievement. Formally speaking, it is just as consistent with this conception to concentrate resources on those with very low levels of talent and motivation, in order to produce more equal levels of achievement across the board.

This conception, as stated, is problematic in various ways.[9] Although condemning inequalities of educational achievement that reflect social class, it casts no doubt on the legitimacy of inequalities of achievement that reflect talent. The term "talent" is ambiguous: it may refer either to natural talent or to developed talent, and there are problems on either reading.

One is that a child's socioeconomic background may it-self influence her level of "talent." Suppose we have in mind what John Rawls calls a child's "native endowments." Social class may enter the story in two ways. First, what a child is born with can be influenced by in utero development, which in turn is influenced by maternal health, which is it-self influenced by social class. Second, if talent in this sense is heritable, and if parents in different social classes tend to be unequally talented (as would be expected on the meritocratic view), then children born into families from different classes will themselves tend to have different levels of talent. If by talent we mean developed talents, then it should be obvious how a child's social class may influence those. That aspect of "merit" is in large part endogenous. Whatever a child is born with, as it were, her class background—the resources (both material and cultural) at her parents' disposal, the neighbor-hood she lives in, and many other class-related factors—will immediately start to have an impact on its development.[10]

A further problem with the conception is more funda-mental: what motivates it is the concern that people not be disadvantaged in competitions by characteristics for which they are not responsible. This consideration also condemns unequal achievements due to talent (whether natural or en-dogenously developed) just as much as it condemns those due directly to social class. People are no more responsible for having the talents or defects they were born with than for the class background into which they are born or for the class-based factors that have an impact on their devel-opment.[11] None of these are reasons to *welcome* the fact that social class influences unequal achievement. They are not, in other words, reasons for unease about *educational equality*. Rather, they are reasons for resisting the idea that inequalities of talent (natural or developed) should influence educational achievement. If anything, they support a more radical principle of educational equality, which Christopher Jencks calls "strong humane justice": an individual's prospects for educational achievement may be a function of that individual's effort, but they should not be influenced by her social class background or her level of talent.[12] This conception incorporates the rejection of the influence of social class, but it also rejects the influence of talent because, like social class background, talent is arbitrary. The fairness-based reason for educational equality impugns unequal educational prospects grounded either in social class or in level of natural talent.

I've presented the case for educational equality as a principle of educational justice. Most readers will have balked at some point, for educational equality understood this way might seem implausibly demanding.[13] Consider what a government would have to do in order to ensure equal educational outcomes. Two pervasive influences would need to be counteracted.

First, the family. Parents have unequal educational success themselves, as well as unequal resources, in terms of finances, time, and emotional energy, to invest in their children. So upper-middle-class children simply have much more invested in the development of their human capital outside the school than working-class and poor children do. One well-publicized study in the United States observed that the vocabularies of the preschool children of professional parents in their sample was already larger than that of the *parents* of the children on welfare, and by the age of three those children had heard thirty million more words than the children on welfare.[14] This results in them being better communicators and better able to take up the (often superior, thanks to parental wealth) educational opportunities presented by schools. Their parents have more control over their daily lives, they experience less stress, and they are able to live in neighborhoods with better public health and safety conditions—all factors that affect educational outcomes.

Annette Lareau, in her classic study of social class differences in American family life, *Unequal Childhoods*, discerns different child-rearing approaches between upper-middle-class families, on one hand, and working-class and poor families, on the other.[15] Upper-middle-class parents "actively fostered and assessed their children's talents, opinions, and skills. They scheduled their children for activities. They reasoned with them. They hovered over them and . . . did not hesitate to intervene on [their] behalf. They made a deliberate and sustained effort to stimulate children's development and to cultivate their cognitive and social skills." The working-class and poor parents, by contrast, "organized their children's lives so they spent more time in and around the home, in informal play with peers, siblings, and cousins. As a result, the children had more autonomy regarding leisure time and more opportunities for child initiated play. They were also more responsible for their lives outside the home. . . . Adult-organized activities were uncommon. . . . [T]here was less speech. . . . [B]oundaries between adults and children were clearly marked; parents generally used language not as an aim in itself, but more as a conduit for social life. Directives were common."[16] A recent study shows that in 2005, parents in the top quintile of the income distribution in the United States spent nearly $9,000 per child for enrichment activities such as tutoring, music and athletic lessons, and educational summer camps, more than six times as much as parents in the bottom quintile.[17]

Some of the characteristics that upper-middle-class children acquire as a result of this unequal investment are valuable for advancement only because of contingent features of our society. Trivially, the value of such practices as giving a firm handshake are culturally specific. More fundamentally, as Lareau observes, "this kind of training developed in . . . middle-class children a sense of entitlement. They felt they had a right to weigh in with an opinion, to make special requests, to pass judgment on others, and to offer advice to adults. They expected to receive attention and to be taken very seriously. It is important to recognize that these advantages and entitlements are historically specific. . . . They are highly effective strategies in the United States today precisely because our society places a premium on assertive, individualized actions executed by persons who command skills in reasoning and negotiation."[18] It may even be socially suboptimal that these strategies, or some of them, are highly valued. Perhaps it would be better if more people valued, and displayed, a certain humility and were more oriented toward making themselves valuable to others than toward seeking benefit for themselves. Nevertheless, these traits *are* valued in individualist, competitive, and unequal societies of the kind we inhabit, and as long as parents can spend considerable amounts of time with their children, we should expect that children will achieve unequally unless schools make massively unequal investments in children to offset the effects of these unequal investments in the home—something that is likely to be politically fraught in an unequal society. If we were really determined to eliminate the influence of social class background on educational outcomes, at least in modern individualist capitalist democracies, we would surely have to, as Rawls conjectures, abolish the family.[19]

The second source of persisting unequal outcomes the government would have to counteract is unequal levels of natural ability. Children do not arrive in the world with the same, or even equal, potential for educational achievement at any given level of educational investment, and once they are in the world some acquire impairments; furthermore, some children have sufficiently limited capacities for educational achievement that the only way equality could be reached would be by leveling down. It would probably not be enough simply to reduce public investment in more naturally capable children to zero; more likely, in order to reduce their outcomes to those of the cognitively impaired, for example, we would have actually to impair them. But even severely limiting the investment in other children with more potential would result in society forgoing a good deal of productive human capital.[20]

So a natural response to these observations would be to abandon the idea that equal educational achievement is desirable *at all*. But this is not the *right* response. If we do really have reasons for reducing the influence of social background and talent over outcomes, we can instead say that equality is indeed somewhat desirable but identify other values that particular equality-producing measures would jeopardize or violate, and we can explain why equality is not so valuable that it justifies jeopardizing or violating those values in the circumstances. Consider what it would take to eliminate the influence of social class background on outcomes. In order to fully achieve equality, one measure we would need to take would be the abolition of the family, so that parents would be unable to invest unequally in their children. The family, though, is valuable both for children and for parents, and its value is sufficiently important that it would be wrong to compromise it for the sake of equality.[21] Nevertheless, measures that would bring us closer to equality without undermining the value of the family—such as taxing private school tuition, placing high-quality early childhood education centers in neighborhoods with high concentrations of disadvantage, providing some degree of compensatory funding, lengthening the school day, and establishing professional development programs focused on improving instruction for low-income children—are desirable, and in part that is because they reduce educational inequality without doing anything to compromise successful family life.

Now consider what it would take to eliminate the influence of natural talent on outcomes. In order to fully achieve equality, we would need to neglect (or perhaps even deliberately disable) children whose natural talents make them more likely to be much more educationally successful than some other children—leveling down achievement. At least two values are at stake here: valuing the psychological and physical integrity of the individual prohibits us from deliberately disabling the more talented child, and the desirability of a society that produces many social goods efficiently puts a brake on our willingness to level down achievement. In particular, it seems strange to continue to pursue equality after the point where we think leveling down would make even the worst-off people absolutely worse off than under an unequal distribution. The worst-off people in our society will need, over the life course, access to high-quality healthcare, long-term care, and various technologies that provide entertainment and that enable people to do what their bodies alone could not do. So we weigh educational equality against the value of benefiting the less well-off in terms of their prospects for having a rewarding life. Undoubtedly, high-quality education will be part of what the less advantaged need for rewarding lives, but they also need other people in society to be productive, so their interests are not usually well served by a policy of completely leveling down education.

Again, this is not a reason to reject equality as a principle, nor is it a reason to seek a less demanding reinterpretation of equality. Maybe we should still emphasize benefiting less talented students over more talented students, other things equal. The consideration invoked suggests a different principle, one that might sometimes conflict with equality and might sometimes take priority over it. Gina Schouten has proposed another principle for guiding the distribution of educational goods, which I shall call *prioritizing the less advantaged*. She simply puts this principle on the table and does not say how much weight it should have relative to educational equality. This principle is subject to both more demanding and less demanding interpretations. The most stringent version of the principle would demand *maximizing* benefit to the least advantaged, whereas the least-demanding just requires that *some priority* (however little) be given to the less advantaged.[22]

Let us assume the most stringent version. Note that it does not say we should maximize the least advantaged's share of *education*. The preceding discussion invoked the quality of life the less advantaged will enjoy, and acknowledges that sometimes the education of other people—those who are more likely to develop or disseminate life-enhancing technologies or become high-quality caregivers—benefits the less advantaged, such that a concern with the less advantaged should lead us to invest in the education of the more advantaged.

The thought behind prioritizing the less advantaged generally is that society is supposed to work for everyone, and that looking at the least advantaged people is a sensible way of gauging whether it is actually working for everyone. Everyone has a claim against being harmed, but nobody has any claim that society should be set up to benefit *them* more than other people—that is, nobody has a prior claim to deserve better education or a better life than others— so there is no default assumption that social institutions should be designed to benefit people with certain specific talents or characteristics.[23] If the worst-off people in society are better off than the worst-off would be in any other feasible arrangement for that society, then they cannot legitimately complain, because they have no claim not to be the worst-off people. But if *they* cannot legitimately complain about *their* situation, then neither can anyone else, because everyone else is better off than the worst-off, and no one has a claim that arrangements must be designed to make *them* better off.

Notice that I have focused on the absolute condition of the worst-off people—that is, on how well-off they are *all things considered*, rather than on how well educated they are. How well educated people are and how well-off they are all things considered are related in complicated ways. The argument for educational equality—for seeking roughly equal educational outcomes—assumed that education is instrumental for success in labor markets, which, in turn, has an influence on our access to all sorts of valuable things. And that is all true when we think of society and its economy in a static way. But modern societies with market economies are dynamic: how much material wealth and what kinds of opportunities are available, how interesting the median job is, and what kinds of social relationships prevail are all things that change over time, partly in response to human activity. That human activity, in turn, is affected by investments in education—in the development of human capital. And it need not be the case that more investment in education is always better.

I'll explain later why there is a tendency to underinvest in education. But, despite that tendency, there could be such a thing as *overinvestment* in education at the social level. Societies need to devote resources to transportation, other forms of infrastructure such as sewers, medical care, agriculture, even the manufacture of consumer goods. If a society devoted, say, 80 percent of its GDP to educating children, it is easy to imagine that everyone—including the least advantaged—might end up worse off over time because of underspending on other things that bring value to people's lives.

The dynamism of societies and economies means that it is also not the case that each person is always better off if resources are invested in his or her education rather than in someone else's. We all depend for our flourishing on other people—their knowledge and skills and how they deploy them. To give an intuitive example, consider people with severe cognitive or physical disabilities. It is true that when they enter the labor market they will always do better if they are better educated and others are worse educated. But over the course of their lives their flourishing may be facilitated

by the education of people who discover, invent, and disseminate technologies to improve mobility, hearing, vision,
or the social integration of people with disabilities. It is not
implausible that maximizing the all-things-considered benefit to people with disabilities may, in some circumstances,
be better achieved by investing more in other people's education at the margins.

What is true of people with disabilities may be true
of disadvantaged people generally. But what I have said
may be false of both! Whether less advantaged people are
benefited by investing in the education of more advantaged people depends on how society and its economy are
structured. Societies and economies vary not only in how
productive they are but also in how the fruits of that productivity are dispersed. In some societies and economies
the social product is controlled by a small proportion of
the society—sometimes, as in the antebellum South of the
United States, by a section of society that does not actually
do much of the producing itself. In other societies the social
product is more widely dispersed. Statistics on the distribution of income and wealth suggest that the social product
is less widely shared—and shared less to the benefit of the
least advantaged—in the United States today, for example,
than it was in the early 1970s. It also seems to be shared less
to the benefit of the least advantaged in the United States
today than in Sweden. Concomitantly, it is easier for highly
educated people to capture more of the value of the productivity that their education yields in the United States today
than it was in the early 1970s or than it is in Sweden today.

Prioritizing benefit to the less advantaged really focuses
on all-things-considered benefit—how well their lives will
go—rather than just on their labor market prospects or on

their level of education. What exactly it means for the distribution of educational outcomes depends on the social and economic structures they inhabit. In general, in countries with more progressive taxation systems and high-quality mechanisms for redistribution of resources to the less advantaged, we would expect more of the benefits of educating those with highly valued talents to redound to the less advantaged than in countries with less progressive taxation, lower-quality redistributive mechanisms, or both. In that case, it might sometimes make sense to invest more in the education of highly talented people in order to enhance the pool of productive skills that will be put to use for the benefit of all. Even in such societies, of course, people who are themselves disadvantaged still need a reasonable level of educational achievement in order to be self-governing, to be productive, and to contribute to social cooperation.

Fortunately, in the non-ideal societies that most of my readers inhabit, I don't think that we need to know *exactly* what it means for the distribution of educational outcomes. In the contemporary United States in particular, I do not think there is any danger of us adopting policies that lead to overinvestment in education, and I also think it is pretty clear that we underinvest in the education of the least advantaged 30–40 percent of the population. Too, the debate about markets is not primarily a debate about levels of investment in education, but more about how efficiently we use the resources that we do invest.

How do the two principles of distribution I have articulated relate to each other? I don't think the preceding discussion depends on a precise answer to this question, which is a good thing because I am not able to give a precise answer. As a matter of moral urgency, when I think about the two societies I know best, the United States and the United Kingdom, benefiting the less advantaged all things considered seems to matter more than equalizing outcomes, and I think that the criterion of benefiting the less advantaged is probably a more useful heuristic in the circumstances most policymakers find themselves in. Think about what it is like being in the bottom 30 percent of the income distribution and the bottom 30 percent of the labor market in the United States. People in that situation are much more likely than others to be living in neighborhoods where violence, in particular gun violence, is an ever-present threat. They have poor access to basic healthcare, and typically live in rental properties from which they can easily be ejected by the landlord. Their jobs are insecure, often dreary, and usually very poorly paid; they have limited control over the course of their workday; and their line managers have very little incentive to care about or invest in their professional development. Avoiding consigning a student to the stresses of living in those conditions should be a very high priority for an educator, and for those involved in making education policy.

By now it must be clear that I recognize a plurality of values that bear on how education should be distributed. For example, I recognize that the value of maintaining healthy family relationships, or of maintaining the connection of children with their cultures of origin, might sometimes conflict with measures recommended by equality or benefiting the less advantaged, and the value of those relationships or connections might sometimes matter enough to make those measures unacceptable. So considerations in addition to equality and prioritizing the less advantaged matter. But

I think that those two criteria, although they are distinct and can conflict, usually bear similarly on decisions about whether and how to use markets in education.

NOTES

1. Harry Brighouse, Helen F. Ladd, Susanna Loeb, and Adam Swift, *Educational Goods: Values, Evidence, and Decision-Making* (Chicago: University of Chicago Press, 2018.
2. I understand that this is not entirely uncontroversial. In particular, some adherents to some religious conceptions of flourishing may believe that knowledge of other religions is risky, especially in adolescence, because it may undermine continued affiliation to the religion in which the child has been raised. Notably few, however, believe that acquaintance with their own religious commitments and traditions would be damaging to others.
3. See Amy Gutmann, *Democratic Education* (Princeton, NJ: Princeton University Press, 1999); Eamonn Callan, *Creating Citizens: Political Education and Liberal Democracy* (Oxford, UK: Clarendon Press, 1997); Macedo (2000); and Danielle Allen, *Education and Equality* (Chicago: University of Chicago Press, 2016), for a sample of different arguments for the conclusion that promoting democratic competence is an important aim of education.
4. On the practical implications of an educational concern with personal fulfillment, see John Peter White, *Exploring Well-Being in Schools: A Guide to Making Children's Lives More Fulfilling* (London: Taylor & Francis, 2011).
5. Christopher Jencks, "Whom Must We Treat Equally for Educational Opportunity to Be Equal?," *Ethics* 98, no. 3 (1988): 518–533 at 518.
6. This is a central theme of, for example, Clarke (2003) and David Miliband, Minister of State for School Standards, "Personalised Learning: Building a New Relationship

with Schools," speech to the North of England Education Conference, January 2004.

7. See the definition of "weak humane justice" in Christopher Jencks, "Whom Must We Treat Equally for Educational Opportunity to Be Equal?," *Ethics* 98, no. 3 (1988): 518–533.

8. See David C. Berliner, "Our Impoverished View of Educational Reform," *Teachers College Record* 108, no. 6 (2006): 949–995, and Richard Rothstein, *Class and Schools: Using Social, Economic, and Educational Reform to Close the Black-White Achievement Gap* (New York: Teachers College Press, 2004), for nice accounts of ways in which non-education-related reforms might be crucial to improving schools and why addressing child poverty might be especially important. For a rich account of the unequal preparedness of children to deal with school, see David T. Burkam and Valerie E. Lee, "Mathematics, Foreign Language, and Science Coursetaking and the NELS: 88 Transcript Data," NCES Working Paper 2003-01, National Center for Education Statistics, Washington, DC.

9. For fuller discussion, see Gordon Marshall, Adam Swift, and Stephen Roberts, *Against the Odds? Social Class and Social Justice in Industrial Societies* (Oxford, UK: Clarendon Press, 1997), ch. 7.

10. I owe this point to Adam Swift. The endogeneity of "merit" in this sense is emphasized in Elizabeth Anderson, "Uses of Value Judgments in Science: A General Argument, with Lessons from a Case Study of Feminist Research on Divorce," *Hypatia* 19, no. 1 (2004): 1–24, and acknowledged in Adam Swift, "The Morality of School Choice," *Theory and Research in Education* 2, no. 1 (2004): 7–21. See also Elizabeth Anderson, "Fair Opportunity in Education: A Democratic Equality Perspective," *Ethics* 117, no. 4 (2007): 595–622, and Debra Satz, "Equality, Adequacy, and Education for Citizenship," *Ethics* 117, no. 4 (2007): 623–648.

11. See Jencks, "Whom Must We Treat Equally."

12. See the definition of "strong humane justice" in Jencks, "Whom Must We Treat Equally."

13. As pointed out in Jencks, "Whom Must We Treat Equally," which is the classic philosophical discussion of educational equality. For developments in the debate about educational equality, see Gutmann, *Democratic Education*; James Tooley, *Disestablishing the School: Debunking Justifications for State Intervention in Education* (Aldershot, UK: Ashgate, 1995); Anderson, "Fair Opportunity in Education"; Gina Schouten, "Fair Educational Opportunity and the Distribution of Natural Ability: Toward a Prioritarian Principle of Educational Justice," *Journal of Philosophy of Education* 46, no. 3 (2012): 472–491; and Harry Brighouse and Adam Swift, "The Place of Educational Equality in Educational Justice," in *Education, Justice and the Human Good: Fairness and Equality in the Education System*, ed. Kirsten Meyer (London: Taylor & Francis, 2014), 14–33.

14. Betty Hart and Todd R. Risley, *Meaningful Differences in the Everyday Experience of Young American Children* (Baltimore: Paul H. Brookes, 1995).

15. Annette Lareau, *Unequal Childhoods: Race, Class, and Family Life* (Berkeley: University of California Press, 2003).

16. Lareau, *Unequal Childhoods*, 238.

17. Neeraj Kaushal, Katherine Magnuson, and Jane Waldfogel, "How Is Family Income Related to Investments in Children's Learning?," in *Whither Opportunity? Rising Inequality, Schools, and Children's Life Chances*, ed. Greg J. Duncan and Richard J. Murnane (New York: Russell Sage Foundation, 2011), 187–206.

18. Lareau, *Unequal Childhoods*, 133.

19. This point should not obscure the fact that there is a core set of cognitive skills and non-cognitive traits that are likely to be valuable in pretty much any circumstances, at least in advanced technological societies—for example, highly developed computational skills, a reasonable level of self-confidence, the ability to self-regulate without external discipline, and so on—and these traits are easier to develop when more is invested in one's upbringing.

20. Notice that just as some of the socially formed characteristics have marketable value only because of contingent features

of a society, for many natural talents the expected market payoff to developing them varies by society. For example, the relative earnings of entertainers and athletes depend on the level of disposable income and the sophistication and reach of media technologies. To take a different kind of example, sight is essential for understanding and producing the written word in a society that has not developed a technology such as Braille, but blindness need hardly be a barrier at all to understanding and producing the written word with contemporary computer technologies.

21. See Brighouse and Swift, "The Place of Educational Equality in Educational Justice."

22. Schouten, "Fair Educational Opportunity." Obviously, the inspiration for Schouten's principle is Rawls's difference principles; see John Rawls, *A Theory of Social Justice* (Cambridge, MA: Belknap Press, 1971).

23. Schmidtz argues that we can come to have deserved something as a consequence of what we do with it; see David Schmidtz, "How to Deserve," *Political Theory* 30, no. 6 (2002): 774–799. This is consistent with there being no prior claim to a better education.

3

The Ineliminable Role
of Markets in Schooling

I'VE ESTABLISHED THE PARAMETERS WITHIN which I want to think about policy, and the ideals that should guide policy. Within that framework, let's finally start to talk about markets in education.

I want to start by observing that, within the parameters I have assumed, there is no feasible market-free education system. Because opponents of school choice, charter schools, and vouchers sometimes evince very fierce hostility to markets, it is worth understanding just how pervasively market mechanisms affect—and always have affected—education systems in the developed world, and that these market forms are rarely if ever seriously challenged. The most obvious fact is that in all developed countries private schools are legal, and so at least the more affluent parents have a market-based option: if they don't like the public schools that are readily available in their locale, they can choose to exit the public system for the private system, albeit at a cost. In the United Kingdom about 7 percent of school-age children attend private schools; in the United States the figure is roughly 12 percent. In many countries—and especially in the United States—parents with the relevant resources can also homeschool their children. And, again for more affluent parents, even if their child attends a public school, they can supplement with additional lessons, or compensate for low-quality instruction by purchasing tutors and other kinds of educational support in the supplementary educational services market.

Also obvious is the fact that more affluent parents can exercise choice over their children's schooling without ever resorting to exit from the public school system, through decisions about where to live. In the United States and United Kingdom, most children attend their neighborhood schools, and in more affluent areas real estate agents normally include school quality as a major selling point for houses. Less affluent parents typically have less choice: they have fewer resources to spend on housing; if they are in the private rental market—and especially if they have insecure employment—they may have to move in the middle of the school year; and they have very limited choices that do not afford them giving much if any weight to school quality.[1] The housing market, then, has long been a mechanism through which the affluent exercise choice on behalf of their children, and almost no self-styled opponents of markets in education propose to prevent this from happening.

Markets are also involved even in the public education system in less visible and perhaps less obvious ways. Governments must either contract with developers to build schools or must build them themselves using workers hired in the labor market and materials purchased from the private sector. Books, desks, chairs, computers, whiteboards, curtains, power, and all other resources used in the buildings are, ultimately, purchased in the marketplace. But, at least for now, the single most important input into education is labor—the developed and embodied skills of teachers, administrators, advisors, secretarial and custodial staff, counselors, psychologists, and social workers. The labor market thus has a profound effect on the cost and distribution of quality education.

Let's just consider teachers. If salaries in comparable professions increase faster than salaries in teaching, we should expect talented people who might otherwise teach to plan to enter those other professions—to train as nurses, doctors, lawyers, or engineers, for example. And as salaries and working conditions in more affluent school districts rise, we should expect it to become more difficult for less affluent districts to attract and/or retain skilled teachers. Unless society decides to conscript teaching labor in the way that some societies conscript into the military in times of war or insecurity, the labor market influences the quality and the distribution of educational opportunities.

Taking markets out of teaching—that is, conscripting teachers—could radically reduce the cost of education in general, and especially educating the less advantaged, because society could require young people with great potential as teachers to train as teachers, and then allocate more skilled teachers to more disadvantaged students without having to bear the costs of financial incentives. But I take it we generally think that conscripting labor is undesirable except in times of potential catastrophe, both because we think that people should be free to choose among potential career opportunities and because we think the real costs of social enterprises such as educating the next generation should be distributed fairly among all of us, rather than an excessive proportion of those costs being borne by those whose talents happen to suit them particularly well to socially urgent labor.

The thought is not that nothing can be done to improve the quality of the teaching force or to improve the distribution of high-quality teachers among different kinds of students. But the typical proposals for improving the quality of the teaching force and the distribution of high-quality teachers among different kinds of students involve market mechanisms. We propose to pay teachers more and to improve working conditions, so that more talented people will choose to become teachers, or we propose to pay teachers in low-income schools more so that those schools will attract a larger number of high-quality teachers to the jobs they advertise.

Almost nobody, in other words, actually proposes to eliminate markets from educational provision. In fact, nearly everybody accepts that markets must play a considerable role.

NOTE

1. See, for example, Matthew Desmond, *Evicted: Poverty and Profit in the American City* (New York: Broadway Books, 2016).

4

The Case Against Markets in Education

IF NOBODY PROPOSES TO ELIMINATE markets, and everyone understands they must play a considerable role, what on earth is this book about? When we actually debate markets in education, the disputes usually have four analytically distinct but practically connected dimensions.

Contrast two models: the pure government model and the pure private model. In the pure government model, schools are set up and run by a government department, which decides where schools will be located and which children will attend each school, provides all the funding (and disallows any private funding), and regulates principal and teacher licensing, the curriculum, and professional development around instruction. In the pure private model, any organization is free to establish and run a school—a church, a political party, a nongovernmental organization, a corporation, or an individual. Students apply to attend schools, which, in turn, have total discretion over which students they admit. The government provides no funds at all (so all funding comes from a combination of fees paid by the family and private philanthropy), and the government imposes no education-specific regulation (so schools are regulated like other businesses, perhaps to prevent fraud and to ensure health and safety, but there are no licensing requirements for teachers or principals, and no curricular requirements for schools).

I hasten to mention that few activists, politicians, or theorists propose either of these models. Most supporters extending the use of markets in, and privatizing, K–12 education, see some value in governments funding and/or regulating schools, and most opponents see some value in allowing schools some freedom to control their own affairs, including, sometimes, allowing some to have some say over which students they will enroll. The models are for analytic purposes only—ideal types representing the polar extremes within the space that is really in dispute.

The four dimensions on which the two models contrast are the kind of organization that can run a school, the mechanisms through which students are allocated to schools, the source of funding for the schools, and how the schools are regulated.[1] I think it is useful to look at each dimension in turn and explore mechanisms through which the market version might lead us to expect departure from the goals I set out in Chapter 2. Then I shall discuss the ways in which markets in education are unavoidably imperfect and, thus, inefficient. After that I shall look at the evidence we have about market reforms in the United States and, to a much lesser extent, in other countries.

WHAT KINDS OF ORGANIZATIONS RUN SCHOOLS

Let's start with the question of what kinds of organizations run schools. Typically in the United States, control of public schools has been in the hands of school district officials, who hire principals to run the schools and teachers to staff them. The school district officials are governed ultimately by locally elected school boards. In other words, school boards oversee executive decision-makers on behalf of voters.

The introduction of charter and voucher schools has created two alternatives to this model. One is the institution of the independent nonprofit organization that has special tax status; the other is a for-profit private corporation. Under charter legislation, the district or the state contracts out educational provision to the organization, specifying performance metrics; in the case of vouchers, a government entity (usually the state) provides funds on a per-pupil basis, usually with very few strings attached. The organization either owns or rents school buildings and hires management and staff directly. Typically voucher schools operate under very light regulation (on which more later), while the extent and kind of regulation charter schools operate under varies enormously across the forty-two states that have charter legislation.

Some opponents of marketization focus on what kinds of organizations provide schooling. Although I will not dwell on this issue, I think that focus is probably a mistake. It's very hard to provide evidence either way, because most reforms that allow for different forms of provider also alter funding and student allocation rules and other kinds of regulation. But the provision of traditional public schooling in the United States that I have described is very specific to a time and place, and not at all like the way it is provided in some other countries. In the Netherlands, for example, provision has long been mainly by private (usually nonprofit) entities. Most Canadian provinces have separate public school systems for secular and religious schools, and the providers of the religious schools are independent entities connected to churches. Since 1944 churches (and, latterly, other religious organizations) have played a large role in the provision of much public schooling in the United Kingdom, under various arrangements. Even non-church-affiliated schools in the United Kingdom have boards of governors that are partly appointed by the local education authority (school district) and which, along with the principal, hire the staff: the school, rather than the local authority, is the direct employer of teachers. Even before the introduction of charter-like legislation in the United Kingdom beginning in the 1990s, the provision of schooling resembled a mix of the traditional model in the United States and charters. And in the United Kingdom democratic control was not (normally) exercised through direct elections of a school district's board, but through electing a city, district, or county council that has schooling as just one of its responsibilities, and through electing national governments that have jurisdiction over education policy.[2]

ALLOCATION OF CHILDREN TO SCHOOLS THROUGH PARENTAL CHOICE

Now let's turn to how children are allocated to schools. Marketization of schooling is usually associated with parental choice: the idea that parents, rather than the government, should decide which schools their children should attend. It is easy to see how increasing the power of parents to decide which schools their children attend could be at odds with some of the aims and distributive goals I have described. Let's start with the most obvious. I said that personal autonomy—the capacity to make independent judgments about how to live, and to act on those judgements—was an aim of education. But if parents are inclined, as many undoubtedly are, to shape their children's values to be like their own, then they will be inclined to seek out schools that reflect their own values. At the limit this could be disastrous for their children's prospective autonomy. Imagine a child whose parents are left-wing, atheistic, and anti-militarist; the parents can seek a school for their child that embodies left-wing, atheistic, and anti-militarist values, and if sufficient diversity and choice prevails in the local schooling market, most of the other children in that school will have similar values. This is a recipe for the reinforcement of the parents' values, not for the development of autonomy. Where will the child meet teachers who challenge her to reflect on her parents' values? Where will she encounter children raised as Muslims or Christians who will give her a more realistic understanding of the nature of the religious life than her parents (and the mainstream culture) may have presented to her? Where will she encounter children from military families whose parents she might come to know and appreciate, lending nuance to her understanding of the motives and character of members of the military? Schools, when well organized, enable children to explore beyond the boundaries of their families and their communities without forgoing the support those families and communities afford them.

Now consider democratic competence. To become a competent democratic citizen the child of left-wing atheist parents must have an understanding of the values of her fellow citizens who are religious and those who are conservative, so that she can argue with them, so that she can offer reasons for public action that *they* can understand and appreciate, and so that she can learn from them doing the same. A school that is designed to reflect and reinforce her parents' views, and where she does not meet students with different values, is unlikely to facilitate that understanding.

Consider now the distributive goals I outlined. Parents are often motivated to a large extent by consideration of their own children's future advantage, and considerably less motivated by consideration of the advantage of others. So they will go to some trouble to secure positions for their children in schools where their peer group will challenge and support them, and which teachers find it appealing to teach in (because such schools will have a better chance of hiring and retaining high-quality teachers). Families with more cultural capital, more money, and/or more time will be better able to navigate the market. And schools have incentives to attract students who will be less expensive to teach, have more support at home, and will be less likely to disrupt the classroom. In some jurisdictions (in much of the United Kingdom, for example), parental choice is accompanied by selection on the part of schools, which forms a particularly toxic combination: more socially advantaged children cluster together in schools where they have more favorable educational environments, while socially disadvantaged students concentrate in other schools.

Some of these problems can be addressed to some extent by funding formulas and regulations. So in the United Kingdom, where parental choice combines with school selection, the central government enacts a funding formula that results in schools with higher concentrations of disadvantaged students having more money to spend. The establishment of cross-school standards, and an accountability regime that effectively maintains those standards, can go some way toward neutralizing the effects of parents' preferences to shape their children's values: schools can be required to teach in a way that makes it more rather than less likely that children will be challenged to be autonomous and to become democratically competent. Schools could be given financial incentives to attract students from a mix of socioeconomic backgrounds, a mix of cultural backgrounds, and a mix of religious backgrounds. In the United States, charter schools are not allowed to select students, but if they are oversubscribed, they have to use a lottery to determine which students to admit; the largest voucher system in the United States also uses lotteries for admissions.

We'll talk more about funding and regulation in a moment. But it is worth noting some of the limitations of funding and regulation in affecting the allocation of children to schools. For example, it is difficult to know how much funding is needed to compensate for concentrated disadvantage; the amounts used in the United Kingdom and in the Netherlands seem not to be based in any sort of science, and large achievement gaps persist. The larger the amount needed, furthermore, the more politically difficult it is to enact legislation ensuring it. And we have reasons to be skeptical that autonomy and democratic competence can be secured through curricular measures alone. No curriculum is teacher-proof; a school populated by reliably left-wing, reliably racist, or reliably Christian teachers, with an ethos to match, could probably reinforce children's attitudes even if it uses a formally challenging curriculum, and it is hard to imagine that a polity allowing for that degree of parental choice would devise valid measures of learning that picked up on the attitudes characteristic of autonomous and democratically competent citizens. More significantly, I am personally skeptical that deep learning about ways of life other than one's own can reliably be achieved without regular embodied exposure to, and engagement with, people who are raised in and/or committed to those ways of life. The thought is not at all that diversity *suffices* for such learning—we have ample experience suggesting otherwise—just that it is normally *a precondition of* such learning.

PRIVATIZATION OF SCHOOL FUNDING

Currently, in most wealthy democracies, schooling is free at the point of delivery: parents do not have to pay more than a nominal sum to send their children to public schools. *Fully* subjecting schooling to market forces would remove this funding. The government would simply stop paying anything toward schooling, and funding would be entirely up to families and philanthropists.[3]

I think it is easy to see how a system without government funding would fall short of the distributive ideals I have described, and also how it would probably fall short on some of the aims of education. Advocates of complete defunding are, as I'll indicate, rare, but I think it is fair to say that they advocate not merely withdrawing funding for education but also lowering taxes, so that families would be left with more money to pay out of pocket for schooling: and they argue, rightly, that most families would be motivated to ensure that their children got some education. Still, it is easy to see why the less advantaged would be less well educated under those arrangements not only than they would be ideally but also than they are now. Most wealthy countries engage in progressive taxation—those with higher incomes pay more—so reducing taxation may benefit more affluent families more than those with lower incomes. Those families would then have more to spend than lower-income families, and, assuming that parents are primarily interested in the future prospects of their own children, they would spend that money accordingly. Of course, regulation could attempt to ensure that the children of the wealthy and the poor share the same schools and the same classrooms but, again, it is hard to imagine a polity that does not fund schooling wanting to enact such regulation. It is much more likely that the children would attend separate schools, in which we would see a concentration of more affluent children in well-funded schools and of lower-income children in worse funded schools, and there's no reason to suppose that philanthropic funding would be able to offset this effect. Better-funded schools, enrolling children who face fewer barriers to learning, will generally outcompete worse-funded schools for high-quality teachers: as a general rule, workers who are in demand will prefer higher wages and better working conditions if they can get them. Removal of government funding would worsen the situation of the less advantaged relative not only to the ideal but also to the present day.

As I said, proposals to remove the government *completely* from funding of schools are rare. The movement toward marketization in the United States, as in the United Kingdom and other wealthy countries that have experienced it, has maintained government funding, albeit arguing that private entities will use the funds more productively. This reflects, to some extent, the intellectual origins of the movement: in his classic chapter on markets and education in *Capitalism and Freedom*, Milton Friedman argues that the government should withdraw from the provision and regulation of schooling, but not from funding it.[4] He argues that education has certain civic benefits, which in the absence of public funding would be undersupplied, and he hazards that the government would need to spend about a third of what it did at the time in order to ensure the supply of those benefits. He might not be right about the amount, but parents concerned exclusively with their children's future prospects have good reason to underinvest in their becoming competent democratic citizens and in their developing the skills that will make them socially productive. The main beneficiary of competent citizenship is not the citizen herself but those with whom she interacts—those who are on the receiving end of her thoughtfulness, reasons, and self-restraint. Those with socially productive skills are sometimes well rewarded, but often less well rewarded than they would be if they have less socially productive skills (compare the salaries of primary care doctors with those of plastic surgeons, or those of nurses with those of lawyers). Most of us are worse off if there is an undersupply of good citizenship and socially productive skills, but individually we are better off pursuing our own interests. Government funding, as Friedman recognizes, can solve the collective action problem.

REMOVING GOVERNMENT REGULATION

As I've indicated, regulation could, at least in principle, deal with some of the deleterious effects of parental-choice-led allocation of children to schools, and of withdrawing government funding. But the pure market proposal is to withdraw government from the business of regulating schools. Of course, it would regulate schools the way it regulates other businesses (preferably, for most market advocates, lightly). But it would not engage in education-specific regulation; it would not try to influence the allocation of children to schools, whether schools select students, how much teachers are paid, whether teachers or principals need special licenses, what is taught in schools, how long the school day is, how many days children attend school, or at the limit, whether children attend school at all.

I want to make two, quite different, points about regulation. The first is that, for many of the reasons we have already seen, it is hard to imagine the ideal achievement of the aims and distribution I have outlined without some degree of regulation. Decisions about what organizations will run schools, how children are allocated to schools, and how much funding to give and on what basis are, obviously, regulatory decisions themselves. But even imagining that decisions about those matters are optimal for the goals we have set, for those goals actually to be met, teachers would need to be highly skilled in quite specific ways and would need guidance concerning curricular matters and instructional practices; schools would have to be prohibited from charging excessive additional fees to parents; the length of the school day and the school year would have to be reasonably uniform across schools and districts. Complete withdrawal from regulation seems unlikely to facilitate the goals of Chapter 2.

The second point I want to make is that defenders of government regulation should not, in general, be criticized for defending existing regulations (and defenders of regulation should oppose many regulations). Let's look at some concrete examples. In some US states superintendents of school districts are required to hold advanced degrees—a PhD, EdD, or equivalent. In many states principals are required to hold a license, which can only be acquired by going through some number of semesters of postgraduate education. Many districts have regulations that separate the teaching and management roles, so that one cannot simultaneously be a teacher and a manager. Enthusiasts for markets sometime call for the elimination of these requirements, and I think they are right to call for their elimination. Requirements that superintendents and principals hold advanced degrees or licenses that require considerable postgraduate education, like the forced division between teaching and management, artificially restrict the (already limited) supply of talent to management and leadership and, in particular, make it difficult for the best classroom teachers (who are the most likely to understand the instructional mission of the school, and are least likely to have much spare time to take further college courses) to make the transition into management and leadership. Requirements that teachers be paid and promoted based only on their years of service and qualifications, rather than on the basis of the quality of their work, invite skilled teachers who can find more lucrative employment to do so (and inflates the salaries of less skilled teachers, thus making them less likely to be able to find higher-paid employment outside of teaching). We have good reasons to eliminate *those regulations*, not to eliminate *regulation*.

MARKETS AND EFFICIENCY

I've claimed that in order to approximate the ideal, the government would have to (more or less fully) fund and regulate schooling, and control the allocation of students to schools. In other words, a pure market approach would be very unlikely to approximate the ideal in any reliable way. But few enthusiasts for markets advocate a pure market approach; I've already mentioned, for example, that the pioneer of the market approach in the United States, Milton Friedman, did not initially advocate the elimination of government funding. Market enthusiasts argue instead for the injection of market mechanisms into a public schooling system, on the grounds that doing so will make schooling more efficient.

Before casting doubt on the idea that market mechanisms are liable to generate a great deal of efficiency, I want to make two observations about inefficiency: the first being that it is bad, the second being that it is real.

Defenders of public education as we know it often associate arguments about inefficiency with hostility to public education, and are therefore resistant to and defensive against such arguments; sometimes they even distrust the very concept of efficiency. The distrust of the concept is partly due to a misunderstanding. Seeking efficiency gains is not a matter of looking for ways to reduce spending. The claim that a system is inefficient is just the claim that the value the system currently produces could be produced at a lesser cost, and that at the current cost it could produce more value, if, in each case, certain feasible changes were made. Inefficiency in producing value is always bad, because wherever inefficiencies prevail, value is forgone. If we could reduce spending on the school system without losing value, that would free up resources to be spent on prenatal or postnatal health, or on care for the elderly. If, without spending more, we could implement changes that would result in more educational success, we should do so, because that would enhance the pool of productive skills available to society.

So we should not eschew a concern with efficiency. Some defenders of public education, though, just deny that schooling is inefficient. Claims about inefficiency always involve counterfactuals. A system is only inefficient if some alternative, more efficient way of running it is genuinely feasible, and feasibility claims are hard to vindicate, so it is often difficult to provide compelling evidence. So let us start by considering a situation that many teachers will identify with: the provision of continuing professional development. Many schools have dedicated professional development days at the start of and scattered throughout the school year and school and district officials make choices about what to do on those days. If you talk to teachers about what happened on their last professional development day, many will dismiss what happened as a waste of time: "We'd have been better off working as a team, discussing our grading practices or curriculum, or helping the new teachers with their lesson plans." In saying that, they are identifying an inefficiency, because they are claiming (rightly or wrongly) that something else that clearly was feasible would have contributed more to their collective productivity as teachers than what actually happened.[5]

I've already indicated what *I* suspect are some inefficiencies in American schools—the licensing requirements around principals and superintendents, the bar in many schools on simultaneously having a role as a manager and one as a teacher, and, as the previous paragraph suggests, the way that continuing professional development is organized. I could offer a much larger menu of putative inefficiencies, and different people would have different views about whether they were, in fact, inefficiencies: the disagreements would sometimes focus on whether putatively better alternatives are really feasible, and sometimes on whether putatively feasible alternatives are really better. But the burden of this section is to elucidate some reasons why it is a mistake to expect that market reforms will, as a rule, eliminate efficiency problems.

Perfect markets are perfectly efficient. But markets in schooling are, intrinsically, highly imperfect.

1. Schools have to be above a certain size in order to be viable, not only because teaching labor is expensive, but also because part of what children are learning is how to interact productively with other people. And distance from school matters—people differ in how tolerant they are of long periods of travel, but more than two hours of commuting time will seem excessive to families that have a choice, especially

if transport is not provided and especially when children are young. So outside of very densely populated cities, any family has a limited number of providers from which to choose. By contrast, for many other kinds of service, like plumbing or haircutting, normal market conditions can provide numerous options. The intrinsically limited supply is a serious market imperfection.

2. Once the child is at a school, considerable costs (to the education of the child) are associated with moving her. Different schools and different classrooms move at different paces. A new child has to catch up with the curriculum; the teacher has to get to know her in order to educate her well; she has to make new friends when friendship networks are already cemented; at the very least, she has to get used to the tempo and feel of the classroom. Imagine that a new hairdressing salon opens to compete with your hairdresser. If the new hairdresser is a little better at the same price and you have no loyalty, there is no cost at all to switching. If a school opens that is slightly better than your school, even if you have no loyalty, it would be rash to move a child who is already enrolled in the existing school. Of course, it would make good sense to move from a dreadfully bad school to an excellent school. But that will rarely be the option in front of you: it will, as in the case of other services, be more common to face a choice between one provider and another that is somewhat, but not enormously, better.

3. Perfect markets depend on well-informed firms and well-informed consumers. The problem with schooling is that the information a parent needs in order to make a good choice is highly individualized and is difficult to obtain. Some who argue for markets say that parents know their children best and are more motivated than other involved parties by the interests of their children. This is usually true, but the information they need in order to make a good decision—the quality of decision that, when made by numerous market actors, really imposes the discipline of the market effectively—includes information about the quality of the school, which is hard to find. Most schools in OECD countries are now required to publish data on various kinds of achievement. But the achievement level of the students in the school is never a measure of the quality of the education in the school. For that you need high-quality "value-added" measures, which tell you something about the quality of *learning* in the school—for example, comparing the achievement of children before they attend the school with the achievement of the same children after they attend the school.

The problem is not only that we do not have well-developed value-added measures for comparing schools. Harvey Goldstein explains:

> Schools cannot be summarized by a single value-added score—they are differentially "effective" for different kinds of pupil and in different subjects. . . . More seriously, the

numbers are smallish so that sampling error gives you very wide uncertainty intervals and this means that for anything between 60 and 80% of schools they cannot be distinguished from the overall average! Some schools do turn up as extreme but will not all do so over time, and it is also very difficult to detect schools that are changing consistently over time. In other words, for most schools, there is no statistically valid way they can be ranked.[6]

4. In the passage just quoted, Goldstein has English and Welsh schools primarily in mind, and in England and Wales schools are typically considerably smaller than those most children attend in the United States. A secondary school (serving eleven- to eighteen-year-olds) might have 1,000 or 1,200 students, whereas in the United States a high school (typically serving fourteen- to eighteen-year-olds) will often have 2,000 or more students. So what Goldstein says about uncertainty intervals might be less of a concern in the United States. However, having larger schools exacerbates another problem I have already identified: the paucity of providers among which to choose. Additionally, though, although it is perhaps easier to judge the relative average performance of larger schools, those schools will contain considerably uneven performance internally. And this is a crucial information problem: what the parents want to know, in order to make a good choice, is not how good the school is, but how good the school will be *for their particular child*. Knowing that one school does *somewhat* better on average on most measures (in math, literacy, social studies, modern languages,

music, art, chemistry, and so on) does not give you reason to suppose it will be better *for your child*.

5. The considerations elucidated in points 3 and 4 mean that, on the whole, parents are not great choosers for their children, despite being well informed about their children and motivated on their behalf. What makes matters worse is that choosing schools is not something that one does frequently. Whereas you might visit grocery stores once or twice a week, get an oil change five or six times a year, and even purchase a car every five to seven years, most Western families in a well-elaborated choice system would only choose an elementary school once or twice per child, and a secondary school once or twice per child. The opportunities to improve as a chooser are limited.

6. The quality of the service schools provide is, in part, shaped by the composition of the student body. Think for a moment about higher education: people are eager to attend Harvard, Oxford, the University of Wisconsin–Madison, the Ohio State University, or the Sorbonne, in some measure because of the *other students* they are confident will also be attending. This is partly because one of the purposes of higher education is networking: students want to become part of networks of other successful people, because they believe (rightly) that it will enhance their success. But it is also partly because of who else will be in their classrooms: they will learn from other smart, attentive, dynamic students, and from the interactions between *those* students and their common instructors. The same

is true at the compulsory stages of schooling: a school with very few disruptive students, or with very few students with special resource needs, or with many well-prepared and moderately confident students, can offer a better education, other things equal, than a school with many disruptive students, many students with special needs, or few well-prepared students. So schools have an incentive to select their own students and, in particular, to repel students who will be difficult or costly to teach or whom parents of students who are less difficult or costly to teach will want to avoid. In a system in which schools control admissions, the incentives are to discriminate against the students who are most in need of high-quality education. If they concentrate into schools nobody else wants to attend, that raises the costs for (or lowers the effectiveness of) those students.

This is not just a problem for distributive justice. It is also a matter of efficiency: when firms can select their customers and are attractive to their customers for reasons that are independent of their productivity, in imperfect markets this lowers the market pressure for them to improve their productivity. With respect to higher education, in an explanation of why selective colleges and universities persistently fail to attend to improving the quality of instruction (and hence the amount of learning), Robert Zemsky, Gregory Wegner, and William Massy put the point as follows:

> As the admissions arms race has made clear, critics of higher education, and to some extent higher education itself, have

misunderstood the core business of these institutions. Whilst most believe the task of universities and colleges is to supply quality educations at reasonable prices, their real business is to sell competitive advantage at necessarily high prices.[7]

Just to be clear, these intrinsic market imperfections do not mean that markets in schooling would be less efficient than government-provided schooling, or less efficient than schooling as it is currently organized and regulated. Whether or not they would be more or less efficient depends on all sorts of contingencies, including how efficient government schooling is or feasibly could be. Instead they alert us to be cautious of theoretical claims that markets promote efficiency in schooling, and encourage us to scrutinize the evidence.

THE EVIDENCE ABOUT CHARTER SCHOOLS

Most commentators date the introduction of markets into schooling to the late 1980s, when the United Kingdom introduced a limited system of parental choice that pervaded England and Wales. In the early 1990s countries as diverse as Sweden, Chile, and New Zealand introduced limited market-based reforms. In 1991 the Milwaukee Public Schools in Wisconsin introduced a school voucher system that has since been copied (with some variations) in other parts of the United States. The first charter school legislation was passed in 1992 in Minnesota and California; forty-two states now have charter school legislation, under which specific schools fall under different regulations from the regular public schools, are usually operated by nonprofit or (much less commonly) for-profit organizations, and take students on the basis of parental choice, using lotteries to select students when oversubscribed.

Before surveying some of the evidence on these policies, it is worth noting that none amounts to anything like full marketization. In the cases of voucher and charter schools the government pays most or all of the costs of schooling. Most schools in the United Kingdom and New Zealand, and charter schools in many states, are required to adhere to national or state curricular standards, and have to abide by licensing requirements for teachers. Charter schools, and schools in many of the voucher systems, do not get a free hand in choosing which students to serve, but have to select by lottery. So market enthusiasts could, of course, dismiss evidence about these modest market reforms as irrelevant. After reviewing the evidence I shall explain why I don't think that is a good response.

So let me summarize some of the evidence. The most widespread market reform in the United States has been the emergence of charter schools. It is also the reform on which we have the best evidence because charter schools have three features that, together, make them easier than many other reforms to study. First, they are often required to report results on the same tests as students take in the schools with which they compete. Second, they usually do indeed compete with other schools, so there is a local comparison class. And third, oversubscribed schools hold randomized lotteries to determine who gets admitted. These lotteries enable statistical comparisons between students who "lost" the lottery with those who "won" (were admitted to and subsequently attended the charter school). Despite important limitations—for example, these studies are strongly internally valid but only weakly externally valid, since results might not be applicable to charters that are not oversubscribed—these comparisons provide some useful data about the likely effects of the schools.

In 2013–14 there were 6,440 charter schools in operation in the United States (compared with 1,542 in 1999–2000), serving 2.5 million children (compared with 350,000 in 1999–2000). A total of 28.7 percent of charter school students were black, and 28 percent were Hispanic (compared with 15.2 percent and 23.6 percent, respectively, of traditional public school students); charter school students were slightly more likely than traditional public school students to be poor, and slightly less likely to have special educational needs or be English-language learners. Charter schools are substantially more likely to be located in cities than in suburbs, towns, or rural areas, and are disproportionately located in the South and West.

The evidence on charter school achievement effects suggests that they are not, on average, better than traditional public schools in the respects that social scientists measure. One large-scale, lottery-based study, which tracked students who enrolled in lotteries to attend one of thirty-six oversubscribed charter middle schools across fifteen states, found that, on average, charter schools were no more successful than traditional public schools as measured by growth in student achievement on state reading and math tests.[8]

Despite some variation in results, depending on how disadvantaged the students in the school were and whether the school was located in an urban or a rural area, the charters studied had an insignificant or negative impact on student achievement on reading and math state assessments. While charters in urban areas or serving more disadvantaged students had more positive effects (or fewer negative effects) than the other schools studied, the study reported that even these apparent positive effects likely reflected differences in the quality of the educational alternatives available to the control group of students who entered but lost the lottery: disadvantaged students who lost charter school lotteries were more likely to end up in lower-quality non-charter schools than more advantaged students who lost charter school lotteries.[9]

Other research has used longitudinal data to track the academic performance of students as they moved between charter schools and traditional public schools. Examining data from two states and five large urban school districts, Ron Zimmer and colleagues find mixed results for charter school effects.[10] On the whole, when they compared math and reading scores of students attending charters with the scores of those same students while they attended traditional public schools, the study found that students performed similarly across the two settings in most locations. While student impacts varied considerable across schools, attending charter schools appears not to have benefited students on average.

A CREDO study released in 2013 covered about 80 percent of all charter schools in twenty-seven states and the District of Columbia and found more positive results. It concluded that the positive impact of attending a charter school, as compared to a traditional public school, was equivalent to seven days of learning in reading skills. No growth in math skills was found. Some demographic differences were found; for example, low-income black and low-income Hispanic students experienced greater than average growth. A 2009 study using the same methods (but including fewer states) found the charter schools being outperformed by traditional public schools in math gains.[11] And both studies showed a great deal of variation *between* states (i.e., in some states the traditional public schools compared very favorably with the charter schools) and among schools *within* states.[12]

The evidence is not that charter schools are worse than traditional public schools. And the reader should be aware of the evidence that, based on very high-quality studies harnessing the lottery feature to do quasi-experimental research, one specific kind of charter school—what I refer to as "high commitment" charter schools, exemplified by the Knowledge Is Power Program charter management organization—seems to have significant positive effects for the low-income, mainly minority, children who attend. I shall discuss these schools briefly later in the chapter.[13] But my claim is neither that extending markets further into schooling generally makes things worse (it may or may not; the evidence is not conclusive) nor that there is never a case for extending markets further into schooling (although the evidence is not conclusive, I think there sometimes is). It is that, at best, extending the use of markets will not improve things much, and that better public policies are available for improving the extent to which the goals elaborated in Chapter 2 are reached.

THE EVIDENCE
ABOUT VOUCHER SCHOOLS

Now let us turn to some of the evidence concerning vouchers. In 2015–16 there were twenty-three different publicly funded voucher programs operating within the United States. They vary a great deal in the populations they target and serve, the regulations they operate under, and in size: in 2015 Mississippi's two programs enrolled just 150 students between them, and 149 of them were in one program. Altogether, the twenty-three programs accounted for just over 150,000 students: vouchers were still, twenty-five years after the first program opened, a very small part of the educational landscape. Just a few programs—naturally, the larger and more politically salient programs—attract most of the scholarly attention.

Studies of the academic effects of the programs tend to focus on test score growth and high school graduation rates. Whereas the lottery feature enables researchers to do experimental studies on the effects of charter schools, many voucher programs do not require the use of lotteries, so researchers have to use other techniques such as matching (in which they pair participants in the program with non-participants who are as similar to the participants as possible, and compare their progress). As with charter schools, test scores and graduation rates may not capture everything we have reason to care about in terms of educational outcomes—for example, they do not necessarily tell us much about the development of democratic competence or personal autonomy. And the non-experimental nature of some of the research should make us additionally cautious in our interpretation of the results. With that caveat, the research does not support optimism or enthusiasm about extending markets into schooling.

The Milwaukee Parental Choice Program is the oldest program in the United States, dating from 1990, and one of the largest, currently enrolling about 28,000 students. Initially based in the city of Milwaukee, in 2011 it was expanded to include the rest of Milwaukee County, and voucher programs have been set up in other Wisconsin cities. It also has been extensively studied. And the results are significant for our purpose because a much higher proportion of students use publicly funded vouchers to attend private schools in Milwaukee than in any other city: public school students outnumber voucher students by only about 3:1. Early studies in the 1990s, when the program was much smaller and did not include religious schools, suggested some reason for optimism regarding its effects on test scores, but the effects never looked large.[14] Another study found that over a three-year period in the 2000s achievement growth among third through eighth graders in the voucher schools was similar to matched students in the Milwaukee Public Schools.[15] One study sought to explain the apparently small size of the effect in the 1990s by arguing that the competition introduced by the voucher system was having an effect throughout the school district, finding that during the period 1998–2000 test scores grew throughout the Milwaukee schools more than in comparable districts in Wisconsin.[16] A subsequent study, however, found no similar effect in the subsequent two years, and in fact test scores subsequently fell.[17] Carnoy compares eighth-grade math test scores in thirteen cities in 2009, 2011, and 2013. In a comparison group including Houston, Philadelphia, Baltimore, Miami, and Chicago, the scores for Milwaukee were lower than for any other city but Detroit.

Ohio's EdChoice program started in 2005: initially eligibility was restricted to students from public schools the state deemed as low-performing, though in 2013–14 it was opened up to all economically disadvantaged students in Ohio. Because it does not use lotteries (so the private schools receiving the voucher can choose among applicants), research has had to use matching techniques, in which participants are compared with similar students who do not use the voucher. A rigorous study of the program notes three main findings. First, it found that although the recipients of the vouchers were disadvantaged relative to the student population in Ohio, they were not among the *least* advantaged—participants were more advantaged on average than the group of students who were eligible. Second, the study found that voucher recipients experienced fewer gains than the comparison group: that is, the voucher actually hurt them in terms of test score growth. Third, the researchers tried to assess the possibility that the voucher system had a positive effect on the public schools with which they were competing, and in line with the first (but not the second) study of the competitive effects in Milwaukee, they found that the students in public schools did, in fact, benefit somewhat from the competitive effects on the public schools; in other words, they judge that the public schools improved slightly in response to the threat of the voucher schools.

Lowering of test score growth was also found in a lottery-based study of the Louisiana Scholarship Program, a voucher program targeting low-income students that began in New Orleans in the aftermath of Hurricane

Katrina, was expanded statewide in 2012, and awarded more than six thousand vouchers in 2014. Researchers observe that many participating private schools had recently experienced serious declines in enrollment, and it is worth noting that, as in the Milwaukee program (but unlike some others), the schools are prohibited from charging any fees to top up the voucher: the voucher must be accepted as full payment for the school place. Research on the Indiana Choice Scholarship program, a large statewide voucher program that, unusually, does not target disadvantaged students specifically but is used also by middle-class families, also suggests that recipients' test scores suffer relative to matched students who remain in the public schools. Studies of the DC Opportunity Scholarship Program, funded by the federal government for students in the District of Columbia, do not show test score losses, but they do not show test score gains, either, although they do show small increases in high school graduation rates.

HIGH-COMMITMENT CHARTER SCHOOLS

When presenting the evidence about charter schools I promised to discuss one particular kind of charter school—what I call high-commitment charters (HCCs), exemplified by the Knowledge Is Power Program (KIPP) schools. In the public debate about charter schools there is an unfortunate tendency for proponents of charters to cherry-pick successes and for opponents to cherry-pick failures. As we've seen, on average charters perform roughly similarly to traditional public schools: individual successes and failures are just part of the variation you'd expect from any schooling system. If, however, some species of charter school can be shown systematically to perform above average, it is entirely legitimate to point that out, not as evidence in favor of charter schools generally but as evidence in favor of that particular species of school.

These schools are "high-commitment" in several senses. From students, they demand commitment to excellent behavior, large amounts of time devoted to schoolwork both in and outside school, and a commitment to the culture of the school even with respect to practices that contrast with students' home and community culture. From parents, they demand a commitment to the academic and cultural mission of the school, often formalized in a contract backed by the threat of expulsion. From teachers, they demand long hours, far exceeding the time commitment of teachers in standard public schools, and evidence of success in the form of test score gains. Teachers are expected to visit students' homes and monitor their individual progress; they have an unusual level of instructional support from principals and extensive collaboration with peers. While these characteristics are present in various types of schools, HCCs stand apart because of the degree of commitment they demand of the various parties and because this level of commitment is a crucial component of their educational mission and is credited for the academic gains they appear to provide their students.[18]

KIPP schools, whose students are overwhelmingly from disadvantaged backgrounds, appear to improve test scores, graduation rates, and college enrollment. Two recent reports by Mathematica Policy Research, which exploit the use of lotteries for the purposes of getting experimental results, study the effects of KIPP middle schools throughout the country.[19] Both find evidence that KIPP schools produce "positive, statistically significant, and educationally substantial" achievement gains among students who attend them.[20] While the first examines only math and reading achievement on standardized tests, the second is more comprehensive, finding strong gains in reading and math as well as science and social studies. The researchers state that by the third year after enrollment, the average KIPP middle school had produced student gains in achievement equivalent to approximately 40 percent of the local black-white test score gap in math, 26 percent of the gap in reading, and a third of the gap in science and social studies. These gains are manifest not only on high-stakes standardized state tests but also on a nationally normed low-stakes test that attempts to measure higher-order thinking skills. This suggests that the achievement gains that students make in KIPP schools may be generalizable beyond the discrete skills measured in high-stakes tests.

Does the success of *a certain kind* of charter school suggest that markets can be much more successful than they have been? I don't think so. KIPP schools operate at the margins of the systems they inhabit, and there are good reasons to be skeptical that they could achieve what they do if they were placed at the center of those systems. They rely on attracting very talented teachers and administrators who are willing to sign on to the school's mission and devote themselves fervently to the education of disadvantaged students. Highly capable educators are attracted by the prospects of working with other talented and devoted practitioners. The schools appear to rely heavily on young teachers who have not yet started their own families.[21] Educators willing and able to meet the demands of HCCs are a scarce resource. KIPP and other successful similar schools rely, to some extent, on additional funding from the private sector and from philanthropic sources. Since this supply of supplemental funds is finite, it is reasonable to doubt that it is large enough to support schools for all disadvantaged students. It is also reasonable to doubt that there is willingness among voters or their representatives to provide a HCC education to all children at public expense. To demonstrate how costly it would be to provide HCCs at scale, consider one aspect of HCCs: the longer school day. Additional instructional time is deemed important to KIPP's apparent successes. Adding just ten hours a week to the regular school day for *all* urban schoolchildren, making their classroom time comparable to what the average KIPP student experiences, would add considerably to labor costs, either for more teachers or for additional hours of work from existing teachers.[22]

For reasons of political will, funding, and a scarce supply of the right kind of teaching labor, KIPP schools will, for the foreseeable future, continue to serve only a subset of disadvantaged students. But there are reasons to doubt that they, and schools modeled on them, could serve all children even if these practical problems could be overcome. Their essential features—and those plausibly linked to their test score gains—are dependent on the subtle exclusion of the most disruptive students by way of such practices as lottery admissions, parental contracts, and expulsion. KIPP schools do not *intentionally* exclude any lottery participants, and studies show that students enrolling in KIPP schools resemble others in their neighborhoods in terms of race, achievement, and income.[23] Nonetheless, selection is involved. Just enrolling in a lottery requires effort and social capital that may effectively exclude many of the most disadvantaged parents—for example, parents without the time or resources to attend required recruitment events or to gather the necessary forms and documents for applications. KIPP, like other high-commitment schools, require parents to sign a contract in order for their children to attend, effectively asking them to "opt in" to their school and "opt out" of the default public school. Meanwhile, by expelling students for behavioral transgressions, administrators effectively require students to "opt in" to the culture and ethos of the school. (Traditional public schools can, of course, expel students, but unlike charter schools, the public school district continues to be under a duty to educate those students, so public schools face various pressures not to expel that charter schools do not.) These mechanisms of lottery enrollment, parental contracts, and expulsion seem important to the success of the schools, but they inadvertently exclude a certain group of students likely to be among the most disadvantaged, disruptive, or difficult to educate. If these subtly exclusionary practices are essential to securing the documented test score gains that KIPP provides, then those schools cannot be brought to scale even if the political will for funding more of them could be mustered. Their success would depend on their ability to exclude students whose inclusion would make their curricular and disciplinary environments impossible to maintain.[24]

None of the above comments are meant, or should be seen, as criticisms of KIPP or similar schools. The point is that their success cannot be taken as evidence that their model will work if adopted much more widely.

CONCLUSION

This has been a chapter of two parts. The first part makes an abstract theoretical case that we should not expect extending markets in schooling to realize the goals that I elaborated and defended in Chapter 3 for two kinds of reason: first, that some of those goals run contrary to the likely motivations of powerful market actors, and second, because even if that weren't the case, we should expect markets in schooling to be highly imperfect in ways that make for inefficiencies. However, that abstract theoretical argument won't do on its own, because the real policy alternative to extending markets is not simply implementing the goals we have but government provision, which we have reason to believe is itself highly imperfect. So the evidence on real efforts to extend markets in schooling matters. The second part of the chapter surveys some of that evidence and suggests that, in fact, efforts to extend markets in schooling in the United States at least have not, generally, improved matters with respect to the goals described in Chapter 2.

The studies that I have surveyed—like many that assess the effectiveness of schools and school reforms—focus heavily on test scores and, to a lesser extent, on graduation rates. It is no criticism of the researchers to note that these are, to say the least, very imperfect proxies for school quality. In fact, after about twenty years of research on vouchers that, in aggregate, was failing to show that vouchers improved test scores, a number of proponents of school choice and vouchers began to argue that improving test scores was never the purpose of school choice. Here's a striking version of this claim, made shortly after a 2010 study failed to provide evidence that the Milwaukee voucher program improved test scores:

> As an advocate of school choice, all I can say is thank heavens for the Milwaukee results. Here's why: If my fellow supporters of charter schools and vouchers can finally be pushed off their obsession with test scores, maybe we can focus on the real reason that school choice is a good idea. Schools differ in what they teach and how they teach it, and parents care deeply about both, regardless of whether test scores rise.[25]

It might surprise readers, after a chapter that seems devoted to dismissing choice, to discover that I have a lot of sympathy with this viewpoint. Whereas I suspect that very large increases in test score gains do tell us something good about a school, especially holding other things constant, small gains, especially in an accountability environment that encourages schools to focus on improving children's test-taking ability, probably do not tell us much. But it matters that families are happier with their children's schooling; it especially matters that disadvantaged families that are subject to extreme stress not be subject to worries that their children are unhappy in school, or unsafe in or on the way to or from school. The argument of this chapter (and my part of this book) is emphatically not that vouchers, charters, choice, or other market mechanisms should have no place in the educational ecosystem. In fact, as my comments about KIPP schools might suggest, I think that restricted charter school and other choice legislation, especially when it targets disadvantaged students, should be part of the armory of educational policy.

I claim instead, that in light of the theoretical reasons I have adduced, and the evidence we have, it is a mistake to expect that extension of markets in schooling to produce much benefit. I also believe, though I cannot prove, that the focus on markets and choice since the late 1980s has had an opportunity cost—it has distracted attention from measures that are more promising. The actual overall effects of extending markets have been neither successful nor disastrous, but I hope to sway the reader toward taking other measures seriously.

I raised earlier the possibility that enthusiasts for markets might distance themselves from the existing reforms and question the relevance of the evidence about those reforms. The state retains a considerable regulatory role in charter schooling, and it plays the main funding role in both charter and voucher school reforms. Sometimes a compromise policy is worse than either of the policies between which it is a compromise. So although charters and vouchers do not represent an improvement on traditional public schooling, perhaps a much more radical market reform—the complete withdrawal of the state from provision, regulation, and funding—would.

This is an unwise response to the evidence for two reasons. The theoretical arguments I gave for markets being unreliable with respect to the goals we should have for schooling stand, and those arguments caution against the kind of idealistic optimism exhibited here. In particular, we have good reasons to anticipate that, absent government activity, and given the likely motivations of parents to benefit *their own* children, markets in schooling will not optimally benefit less advantaged students, and will not optimally serve the public purposes we have reason to demand of schools.

But there is an equally significant reason. I don't believe that demanding that the government remove itself completely from schooling in advanced, wealthy, liberal democratic societies is a feasible option, even in the United States. Education is too politically important, and seen as too politically significant, for democratic majorities to authorize governments to remove themselves from schooling even if that were the best policy (and I think it is *not*). As long as we assume background democratic conditions. I think it is unfeasible to achieve the pure market model. Opponents of charters and vouchers are not entitled to compare them with some idealized public schooling system that perfectly meets the goals I set out in Chapter 2, but must compare them with public schooling that is only as good as we feasibly could make it over a specific time period. Similarly, defenders of markets in education are not entitled to compare public schools as they are with some idealized version of markets, but are required to compare them with market-oriented reforms that are as good as we feasibly could make them within some specific time period.

NOTES

1. Who can run schools, how children are allocated, and the permissible sources of funding are all, in fact, elements of regulation, but they are worth separating out from other regulation for analytical purposes.
2. Notable exceptions being the London School Board (1870–1904) and the Inner London Education Authority (1965–1990).

3. James Tooley proposes this; see his *Education Without the State* (London: IEA Education and Training Unit, 1996). See also E. G. West, *Education and the State: A Study in Political Economy* (Indianapolis, IN: Liberty Fund, 1965).

4. Milton Friedman, *Capitalism and Freedom* (Chicago: University of Chicago Press, 1962).

5. I deliberately do not comment on how often teachers who say such things are right. But anyone organizing a professional development session, however successful it was, will usually come away thinking, "I wish we had done X because then the day would have been (even) better." The inefficiency may have been small, but inefficiency it was.

6. Harvey Goldstein, "The Difficulty of Ranking Schools," *New Economy* 8 no. 4 (2001): 197–198. See also Harvey Goldstein, "Value Added Tables: The Less-Than-Holy Grail." *Managing Schools Today* 6 (1997): 18–19.

7. Robert Zemsky, Gregory R. Wegner, and William F. Massy, *Remaking the American University: Market-Smart and Mission-Centered* (New Brunswick, NJ: Rutgers University Press, 2005), 71.

8. Melissa A. Clark, Philip Gleason, Christina Clark Tuttle, and Marsha K. Silverberg, "Do Charter Schools Improve Student Achievement? Evidence from a National Randomized Study," Working Paper, Mathematica Policy Research, Princeton, NJ, December 2011.

9. Clark et al., "Do Charter Schools Improve Student Achievement?"

10. Ron Zimmer, Brian Gill, Kevin Booker, Stephane Lavertu, Tim R. Sass, and John Witte, *Charter Schools in Eight States: Effects on Achievement, Attainment, Integration, and Competition* (Santa Monica, CA: RAND, 2012).

11. CREDO, *Multiple Choice: Charter Schools in 16 States* (Stanford, CA: Center for Research on Education Outcomes, 2009).

12. CREDO, *National Charter School Study 2013* (Stanford, CA: Center for Research on Education Outcomes, 2013).

13. For extensive discussions of these kinds of charter schools, see Harry Brighouse and Gina Schouten, "Understanding the Context for Existing Research and Reform Proposals,"

in *Whither Opportunity? Rising Inequality, Schools, and Children's Life Chances*, ed. Greg J. Duncan and Richard J. Murnane (New York: Russell Sage Foundation, 2011), and Harry Brighouse and Gina Schouten, "To Charter or Not to Charter: What Questions Should We Ask, and What Will the Answers Tell Us?," *Harvard Educational Review* 84, no. 3 (2014): 341–364.

14. John F. Witte, *The Market Approach to Education: An Analysis of America's First Voucher Program* (Princeton, NJ: Princeton University Press, 2000).

15. Joshua M. Cowen, David J. Fleming, John F. Witte, and Patrick J. Wolf, "School and Sector Switching in Milwaukee," SCDP Milwaukee Evaluation Report #16, School Choice Demonstration Project, Department of Education Reform, University of Arkansas, Fayetteville, 2010.

16. Caroline M. Hoxby, "How School Choice Affects the Achievement of Public School Students," in Paul Hill, ed., *Choice with Equity* (Stanford: Hoover Press, 2002).

17. Martin Carnoy, *Vouchers and Public School Performance: A Case Study of the Milwaukee Parental Choice Program* (Washington, DC: Economic Policy Institute, 2007).

18. See Jay Mathews, "Work Hard. Be Nice," *Education Next* 9, no. 2 (2009): 29–35; Paul Tough, *Whatever It Takes: Geoffrey Canada's Quest to Change Harlem and America* (New York: Houghton Mifflin Harcourt, 2009).

19. Philip Gleason, Melissa Clark, Christina Clark Tuttle, and Emily Dwoyer, "The Evaluation of Charter School Impacts: Final Report," NCEE 2010-4029, National Center for Education Evaluation and Regional Assistance, US Department of Education, 2010; Christina Clark Tuttle, Brian Gill, Philip Gleason, Virginia Knechtel, Ira Nichols-Barrer, and Alexandra Resch, "KIPP Middle Schools: Impacts on Achievement and Other Outcomes. Final Report," Mathematica Policy Research, Princeton, NJ, 2013.

20. Tuttle et al., "KIPP Middle Schools," xiii.

21. Mathews, "Work Hard. Be Nice."

22. Abigail M. Thernstrom and Stephan Thernstrom, *No*

Excuses: Closing the Racial Gap in Learning (New York: Simon and Schuster, 2003).
23. Tuttle et al., "KIPP Middle Schools," xiii.
24. This section draws heavily on Brighouse and Schouten, "To Charter or Not to Charter."
25. Charles A. Murray, "Why Charter Schools Fail the Test," *New York Times*, May 4, 2010.

5

How to Improve Education

I THINK THE FOCUS ON markets during the past twenty-five years of school reform has been a distraction from feasible reforms that could be more valuable. They have been a distraction on both sides: some enthusiasts for markets have neglected reforms that would have done more good, and some opponents of markets have exerted energy in resisting the extension of markets that would have been better spent on promoting alternative reforms. I use this chapter to articulate some of those alternatives. None of the ideas here is original to me: all have advocates within the research and advocacy communities. I draw particularly heavily on the work of Richard Rothstein and of Greg Duncan and Richard Murnane.[1] Some of the ideas have been implemented to some extent: for example, many states have adopted some version of the Common Core State Standards, which provide a framework for both instructional and whole-school improvement. And some will be congenial to enthusiasts for markets who will (rightly) see them as compatible with extending markets.

If market reforms had a record of great success compared with traditional public schooling, the burden on me in this chapter would be considerable: I would have to show that alternative reforms were available that would do a better job than extending markets at improving the quality of education and distributing it better. In fact, the evidence does not point that way. The idea is not to produce a case for original reforms, but to reorient attention toward reforms that hold promise.

And promise is all they hold. The school system is a vast, highly politically constrained industry enmeshed in a complex social ecosystem, much of which is hard to change and can only be changed slowly and over time. Some enthusiasts, whether of markets, standards-based reform, culturally relevant instruction, or "no excuses" schools, have given the impression that they think these are something like silver bullets that can solve the problems of public education. But they are not. There are no silver bullets. Measures and reforms are available, though, that can help us to reduce inequalities, reduce inefficiencies, and thereby improve outcomes.

OUTSIDE THE SCHOOL SYSTEM

Not all children come to school equally ready to learn. Some of the factors that make them more or less ready to learn are predictable and can be influenced by public policy. Poverty, in particular, restricts the capacity of children to learn in school, just as it undermines other valuable aspects of lived experience. Richard Rothstein explains:

> If you send two groups of students to equally high-quality schools, the group with greater socioeconomic disadvantage will necessarily have lower *average* achievement than the more fortunate group.

Why is this so? Because low-income children often have no health insurance and therefore no routine preventive medical and dental care, leading to more school absences as a result of illness. Children in low-income families are more prone to asthma, resulting in more sleeplessness, irritability, and lack of exercise. They experience lower birth weight as well as more lead poisoning and iron-deficiency anemia, each of which leads to diminished cognitive ability and more behavior problems. Their families frequently fall behind in rent and move, so children switch schools more often, losing continuity of instruction.

Poor children are, in general, not read to aloud as often or exposed to complex language and large vocabularies. Their parents have low-wage jobs and are more frequently laid off, causing family stress and more arbitrary discipline. The neighborhoods through which these children walk to school and in which they play have more crime and drugs and fewer adult role models with professional careers. Such children are more often in single-parent families and so get less adult attention. They have fewer cross-country trips, visits to museums and zoos, music or dance lessons, and organized sports leagues to develop their ambition, cultural awareness, and self-confidence.

Each of these disadvantages makes only a small contribution to the achievement gap, but cumulatively, they explain a lot.[2]

If public policy aims to improve the average quality of educational achievement, giving priority to improving the educational achievement of the less advantaged, policymakers would do well to attend to the characteristics of the out-of-school environment the children inhabit. To put it bluntly, sometimes policies focused on what is going on outside the school might be more cost-effective than policies focused on what is happening within the school, because they might ensure that children on average, and poor children in particular, come to school more ready to take advantage of whatever is happening within the school gates. Rothstein's passage gives us some clues concerning what features of the out-of-school environment we might want to focus on.

Reduce Poverty

The first and most obvious focus would be on reducing child poverty. Greg Duncan and Richard Murnane report on two instructive programs developed in the 1990s in Wisconsin and Minnesota. New Hope provided adults from Milwaukee's two poorest zip codes who could prove that they worked thirty or more hours in a week with a range of benefits including subsidized healthcare, subsidized health insurance, an earnings supplement to put them above the poverty line, and, if necessary, a temporary community service job. The program had an experimental design: of the 1,357 applicants, half were randomly assigned to the program, and MDRC, a highly respected research outfit, compared outcomes for the two groups. Families with young children, in particular, benefited considerably from the program, in terms of employment status and family income. More telling for our purposes was a notable impact on educational outcomes. The effect for girls was small, and sometimes not statistically significant, but boys on average scored 33 points higher on SAT-type tests after two years, and teachers rated boys much more favorably on "positive social behavior" and reported fewer disciplinary issues and less frequent behavioral problems. The Minnesota Family

Investment Program, a state program with a similar design that ran simultaneously, was also studied rigorously and showed similar results, indicating that it may be possible to replicate some of the benefits of New Hope on a larger scale even when run by a governmental organization.[3]

These programs are merely suggestive; it would be a mistake to make too much of two moderately successful programs. But we do have plenty of evidence that correlates affluence with educational achievement. Children from lower-income families graduate from high school, matriculate in college, and graduate from college at lower rates than children from higher-income families; as income inequality has steadily increased since the late 1970s so has the achievement gap, however it is measured, between higher- and lower-income students. The PISA reports measure academic achievement in a way that makes cross-national comparisons: in 2009, it found that in each of fourteen countries (including Finland, the United States, and Norway), children in the 95th percentile of socioeconomic and cultural advantage on average outperform children in the 90th percentile, who outperform children in the 85th percentile, and so on, all the way down the scale. This suggests that it is unduly optimistic to rely on schools alone to improve educational outcomes.

Improve Healthcare Provision

Every wealthy country exhibits what is known as a *social gradient of health*: more affluent, better educated people have better health outcomes than less affluent and less well-educated people. Epidemiologists account for this in significant part by appeal to the health-diminishing effects of stress: both income and education help us to avoid stress, because both give us more control over our lives. The passage from Rothstein quoted earlier in this chapter highlights the significance of this for education. Children in homes with more stress and more illness are more likely to be ill themselves. So they are more likely either to miss school because of illness or, despite being at school, to learn less, because illness reduces the ability to focus and concentrate. This has a greater effect on the less advantaged, on average. Of course, one way to reduce the effect would be to redistribute income and wealth substantially, but I have ruled that out as an option. Improving the quality of primary healthcare and reducing barriers for lower-income families to get basic treatment for children experiencing ill health is more feasible. Sometimes, for some populations, spending on cold treatments and asthma medication, as well as on spare eyeglasses (so that children whose eyeglasses are left at home, lost, or broken can see the board), might be more cost-effective than spending on more traditional academic resources (including, perhaps, even on teachers).

Improve Prenatal and Postnatal Medical Care for Poor Children

James Heckman's research on early childhood provision of education and healthcare support and prenatal support to mothers suggests that investment in high-quality interventions can be effective ways of improving outcomes, including measurable educational outcomes, for children, and especially for poor children (who on average have much worse educational outcomes than more affluent children). A randomized controlled study of the Nurse Family

Partnership in Memphis, Tennessee, is instructive. The program offered voluntary prenatal, parenting, and early childhood supports to low-income first-time mothers. The program consists of home visits from professional nurses with at least a bachelor's degree, starting during pregnancy and lasting until two years after birth. The participants' babies had higher birthweight, and researchers found that by the end of the program (when the children were age two) home environments were healthier and the mothers had more positive parenting attitudes and better mental health. Strikingly, "at age six—four years after the program ended—the home visiting program led to improved cognitive skills for both boys and girls, and better socio-emotional skills for girls. Researchers found the positive effects at age six were largely attributable to the program's impact on maternal health and early-life investments."[4]

Improve Early Childhood Educational Provision

The emphasis on choice and markets in schooling has distracted attention from early childhood educational provision. So, ironically, have attempts to blame schools for the "achievement gap." The truth is that children arrive at kindergarten already very different in terms of measured outcomes: children from less advantaged families are already far behind children from more advantaged families when tested on simple numeracy knowledge, numeracy skills, and vocabulary. This should not be at all surprising. As Rothstein points out, less advantaged children have very different education-relevant experiences prior to arriving at school. A famous study by Betty Hart and Todd Risley followed toddlers in forty-two families and found that children in the professional families heard an average of 2,153 words per hour, whereas children from families on welfare heard an average of 616 words per hour. The working vocabularies of the children at age three were, unsurprisingly, very different: children with professional parents had about 1,100 words at their disposal, whereas children of welfare recipients had 500 words. Children from working-class families heard an average of 1,251 words per hour and had working vocabularies of about 750 words.[5]

In light of this study, it may not be surprising that research on high-quality early childhood education shows considerable effects on later educational attainment and subsequent life outcomes. The most deeply studied and best understood early childhood program was the Perry Preschool Project in Ypsilanti, Michigan, from 1962 to 1967. One of the difficulties with studying early childhood education programs is that to a considerable extent what we care about is long-term outcomes, which of course do not show up immediately. The Perry Preschool studies have an experimental character—because admission to the program was through a lottery—and researchers have been able to follow the participating children affected into adulthood and middle age. Participants were all low-income black children, with low performance on IQ tests. They attended the preschool for just two and a half hours a day, and in addition had a weekly ninety-minute home visit from a teacher; each student attended for just one thirty week period. The curriculum was not focused directly on numeracy and literacy, but emphasized play activities that involved planning and collaborative review, so that the children would learn social skills. The earliest measured outcome was an improvement in IQ measurements, but that faded out after third grade. By age fourteen, however, the children were considerably less likely to be enrolled in special education programs, had much higher basic achievement scores, and were assessed as better on a range of social behaviors. They were considerably more likely than the control group to graduate from high school on time and to attend college. By age forty they were three times as likely to own a home, four times as likely to earn more than $2,000 a month, and almost half as likely to have been arrested.[6]

Research on similar programs with more recent graduates, though it doesn't track children so far into their lives, replicates these findings. David Deming's research on Head Start, for example, indicates that it has similar benefits (including the early increase in IQ test performance, which also fades out), though the benefits are smaller, proportional to the lower cost of the intervention.[7] It seems quite likely that, at least for more disadvantaged children, high-quality investment in early childhood education will have better payoffs in educational terms than school choice (with which, I hasten to add, it is compatible).

Some readers might be concerned that I am violating the rules I set for myself at the start of the essay, where I said that non-ideal theorists should set out the parameters within which they are working, and theorize within those parameters. According to some estimates, as many as 40 percent of children in public schools in the United States are poor; at present there is certainly no political will to eliminate or even significantly reduce child poverty. Of course, this may change; many other wealthy democracies have much less child poverty, and less inequality, than the United States. But even if it does not change, measures could be taken to reduce rates of child poverty somewhat and to alleviate to some degree the effects of poverty on children. Evidence from experiments such as New Hope, Gautreaux, and Moving to Opportunity suggests that small increases in family income and small increases in housing stability can affect educational success; it is probably not an all-or-nothing matter.[8] Even if one level of government refuses to or cannot take action, another level of government may be able to. The general point is not to be distracted from trying to influence the out-of-school environment that shapes children's abilities to learn.

INSIDE THE SCHOOL SYSTEM

Some commentators—and, indeed, some educators—criticize attempts to explain low educational achievement by appeal to features of the ecosystem in which schooling is embedded, and particularly by appeal to the toxic effects of poverty on learning; they consider this to be excuse-making. Everybody is able to learn regardless of their background, such criticism goes, and schools and teachers should not "make excuses" for their own poor performance by locating the problem elsewhere. The focus, these critics say, should be on schools, and what schools can do.

The fallacy should be obvious. Explaining and excusing are different activities. Nobody sensible believes that schools cannot make any difference to learning, and insofar as they can make a difference, that is exactly what they should do. They are more likely to be effective, though, if they operate with a clear and accurate understanding of the children they are trying to educate. If a child is hard of hearing, it would be a mistake to attempt to educate her in exactly the same way as a child with normal hearing. Hearing aids or sign language would be appropriate. If a child arrives at school without breakfast, she needs something that a child who has had a nutritious breakfast does not. If a child arrives the morning after a serious nighttime asthma attack (which in the United States is much more likely if she is poor, because low-quality living conditions, stress, and lack of primary medical care all exacerbate asthma), she has different needs than a child who arrives at school well rested. Attention to the stresses of poverty and the conditions children live in neither blames the poor nor excuses the school or the teachers. It is merely sensible. Pretending to teachers that they and the schools they work in can fully counteract the effects of the multiple disadvantages the broader society imposes on poor children is cruel, and a recipe for disappointment and teacher burnout.

But, as I said, nobody thinks that schools can make *no* difference to student learning. So we should attend to those features of the school and the classroom that can improve the quality of the education children encounter when they arrive at school. The market approach hopes that extending the use of markets will engender competition such that low-performing schools go out of business while high-performing schools survive. If so, there'd be no need for reformers or district officials to look for the practices of high-performing schools that explain their success, or work out how to induce other schools to adopt those practices. But I have given reasons for doubting that markets do, or could, work that way. So we cannot avoid that task.

I cannot give detailed prescriptions here, and that is partly because what is required depends on the specific context. But I can articulate some principles that reforms should aim for, and say something about how those principles might apply in specific circumstances.

Preparing Teachers and Principals

Let's start at the beginning. How are teachers initially trained and educated? Teaching is a difficult and highly complex activity. Children come into the classroom with diverse backgrounds, personalities, levels of preparation, and motivations. They cannot learn unless they cooperate, so the teacher not only has to have the skills that enable a motivated student to learn what she is aiming to teach but also needs the skills to induce students to want to do the things that will enable them to learn. The first principle, then, is to *prepare teachers well*.

Most wealthy countries—and all US states—have regulations about teacher licensing: teachers typically need a college degree, to have taken certain education-specific courses, to have observed other teachers, and to have done some practice teaching. Most initial teacher preparation in the United States still occurs in universities, which are accountable for meeting the licensing requirements but not accountable for meeting them *well*. Understanding that becoming a good teacher involves mastering numerous difficult skills, ensuring that prospective teachers observe high-quality veteran teachers, and giving good teachers professional incentives to mentor prospective teachers are essential. Ensuring that the teacher education curriculum is driven by what the students need in order to become good teachers rather than by the interests of professors is important, as is ensuring that teacher education is not used as a revenue source for subsidizing other aspects of a university's mission.

Just as it is important to prepare teachers well, it is important to identify potential high-quality managers and leaders and prepare them well. In 2010, fourteen prominent US school superintendents signed a letter saying that, "as President Obama has emphasized, the single most important factor determining whether students succeed in school is not the color of their skin or their ZIP code or even their parents' income—it is the quality of their teacher."[9] As I've indicated, I have my doubts about that claim—factors such as parental education and income, the quality of health-care, and public health conditions compete with teacher quality for importance, especially when you consider that for any particular child the choice is usually between teachers with very small differences in quality, rather than between teachers separated by a very large quality gap. But even when considering the relative importance of various school factors it is not clear that teacher quality is the primary one. Having high-quality teachers is important, but, as with any other organization, high-quality workers who are poorly led and poorly managed are much less effective than those who are well led and well managed. Frederick Hess reports that one-third of all public school principals in the United States are former gym teachers or athletic coaches. He also reports that some large urban public school districts in the United States do not conduct even regional, let alone national, searches for school principals.[10] Insofar as universities are involved in licensing principals, the problems parallel those of teacher licensing.

An Infrastructure Supporting Continuous Improvement in Teaching and Learning

Schools are complex socially constructed resources. It takes time and expertise to train teachers and school managers: both teaching and managing are crafts, and success in either involves getting numerous micro-decisions per hour right, which in turn requires training, observation, reflection, and experience. A successful school is one in which the skills of many individual teachers are effectively harnessed together by skillful managers and leaders who facilitate continuous professional development and instructional improvement. But such improvements cannot occur in a vacuum; they require a supporting infrastructure.

Think about how you generally learn a new skill or sharpen an existing one, and take learning to play the guitar as our example. The first stages of learning to play the guitar are straightforward: you learn some basic skills and develop some suppleness in your hands and fingers. But if you want to play at all well—not well enough to make a career of it, but well enough to play in front of strangers without embarrassment—you find somebody who already plays well. You watch and listen, reflecting on what they are doing, noting that they do some things you can mimic, and others that you cannot (or cannot at this stage), and you mimic them. You may try to find many good guitarists with different styles, mimicking several as you try to learn how to do specific things, such as very rapid chord changes, changes between chords that require you to move speedily up and down the neck, stretching your fingers for particularly wide chords, different percussive techniques, and so on. You monitor your own performance, of course, but typically you also get one or several other people to monitor your performance, giving you suggestions, telling you that something you think is working isn't, et cetera. Perhaps not for the tiny handful of stunningly talented players, but for most people, including most of those who become successful professionals, this process is iterative and takes many hours of watching, listening, reflection, and practice. Eventually the guitarist develops his or her own style, which will probably resemble another's style or be composed of several identifiable existing styles, or maybe will be noticeably original. But even the highly original player—think of Jimi Hendrix or Richard Thompson—has a large set of skills in common with other, lesser players, which have been developed in much the same way.

Learning how to teach is not different, except in one important way. Good teaching is composed of a very large set of complex skills that are developed through observation, mimicry, reflection, and practice; you do not (usually, even if you are a highly successful professional) learn to be a good teacher without watching others who are successful, mimicking them in various ways, reflecting, adapting the practice to suit you better, and practicing in the presence of observers who can provide feedback. The difference, though, is this: finding the good guitarist to mimic is simply a matter of watching and listening to the performance, whereas however well you listen to or watch the performance of the good teacher, you cannot evaluate it without knowledge that is not readily available—namely, whether, what, and how much the students learn.

But how do we know whether, what, and how much students learn? And, given that one of our central concerns here is improving the quality of disadvantaged students' learning and experience, how do we know specifically what they are learning and from whom? We need measures of learning, which have to be built around common standards and common assessments. Measuring student progress has two quite different purposes. The rhetoric around No Child Left Behind and more recent discussions of "value-added" achievement data have emphasized just one of these purposes: holding schools (and even teachers) accountable for student learning as a condition of federal funding. Let's call this the *accountability* purpose. We are not ill-disposed to this as an instrument of policy making. But there is a quite different purpose for measuring the progress of the student: to enable teachers to find out whether the strategies they are using are successful, and, if not, to identify other teachers from whom they could be learning to be more successful. Let's call this the *professional improvement* purpose.

Standards help to align teaching within and across schools. Common assessments enable the production of valid tests that have a lower per-unit cost and increase the sample size for any conclusions about who is learning what. If you are struggling with teaching quadratic equations to a particular subgroup in your class, then you want to know what strategies others have used to better effect with that subgroup; if you have common standards and assessments, you will find that out more easily, and then you can observe and learn from those strategies.

Some commonality of standards and assessments is required for the development of an infrastructure of professional improvement. They do not make improvement happen, of course; teachers need the time to observe one another and reflect, and they need the managerial support that enables them to use that time well. The infrastructure requires much more than just standards and assessments.

We have good reasons to conjecture that such an infrastructure benefits disadvantaged students particularly. First, more disadvantaged students have, on average, less well-qualified and lower-skilled teachers than more advantaged students have; their teachers have more room to improve, and they therefore stand to gain more from an infrastructure supporting professional development.

Second, when such an infrastructure is absent, as in the United Kingdom prior to 1988 and in the United States today, more advantaged students typically take examinations that do create such an infrastructure, but specifically for more advanced students. In the United Kingdom prior to the creation of the National Curriculum, an infrastructure of this kind was built around exams taken by most students at age sixteen. In the United States the College Board has developed an infrastructure to support improved instruction around the Advanced Placement (AP) exams, which are primarily for children bound for selective colleges. College-bound students thus have proportionately less to gain from the development of a professional improvement structure, to the extent that the courses they take are already part of a professional development scheme.

Third, the information provided by cross-school common standards and assessments enables policymakers to demonstrate more vividly the unequal learning of subgroups. When in-school standards are the only benchmarks for measuring student progress, there is very little transparency: it is easy for schools to fudge the numbers and, by providing less-demanding offerings to some students than others, to give the appearance of similar achievement. But when cross-school common standards and assessment are used, exactly which students are falling behind is more transparent to the outside world, and political pressure to improve the quality of their experience is more likely to be applied.

Rewarding and Supporting Good Teaching

One of the problems that market supporters frequently point to is the difficulty in a traditional public system of removing poor-quality teachers. Teachers typically have some sort of tenure, and in many jurisdictions union representation, so it is difficult to remove them. In many countries—including, for example, the United Kingdom—the typical education career is structured so that those perceived to be better teachers can earn advancement in terms of both responsibilities and pay; in the United States, typically teachers are paid simply according to their years of service and their formal qualifications. One of the clarion calls of market reformers is to fire bad teachers, and one advantage of the market, they say, is that it makes this possible.

But the issue is complex. The United States has about four million teachers at any given moment, and most teachers leave the profession within five years of starting. Few wealthy societies have a large supply of skilled teaching labor waiting to take up the jobs of low-performing teachers. Teaching is not a high-status, high-pay profession, and when countries experience teacher shortages (as they often do after baby booms, or when wages for teaching fall relative to other comparable professions) they have to invest heavily to induce skilled people to enter the profession. This is made more difficult, not easier, if potential teachers believe that the will to fire teachers is widespread. Once they do enter the profession, their resistance to sensible evaluation practices is reinforced if they observe that low-quality teachers are not evaluated effectively during their probationary period.

While it should indeed be made easier in some jurisdictions to fire teachers, the principle should be to find ways of rewarding effective teachers with status and income and to find ways of improving the performance of lower-quality teachers. What changes that requires depends on what is in place in the particular context. In many school districts in the United States teaching and management responsibilities are treated as incompatible. In those districts, creating positions that combine management and teaching (by, for example, making department chairs a formal part of the hiring and evaluation process) would help to create a career ladder, and introducing formal protocols for evaluation of performance that include observations and feedback and would impact pay raises would reward better practice. More generally, introducing the practice of mutual peer observation according to agreed-upon protocols, firewalled from promotion decisions, would create an environment of mutual learning, in which weaker and newer teachers (and stronger and more veteran teachers as well) can improve their skills. Placing professional development firmly in the schools and ensuring that it focuses primarily if not exclusively on concretely improving instruction by improving skills would be an effective way of raising the quality of instruction. National or state standards, such as the National Curriculum in the United Kingdom or the Common Core standards for literacy and mathematics in the United States, provide the backbone for developing an infrastructure for continual improvement of practice, because teachers have guidelines as to what students should be learning, information about what curriculum will support that learning, and a common language for mutual learning: it is easier to identify successful practice and learn from it.

Changing Funding Formulas

Tackling inequality and improving the education of the less advantaged requires spending more money on the less advantaged—maybe considerably more. Spending more money on them is not enough, for money can be wasted if it is spent badly. But it is implausible to think that disadvantaged students—those who are the most difficult to teach because, in general, they face the highest barriers to learning—can be educated to the same level as more advantaged students without additional spending. Imagine yourself as a prospective teacher, deciding between two jobs at the same salary, one of which will be in a school with a 5 percent poverty rate, the other in a school with a 70 percent poverty rate. To the extent that you are self-interested—that is, that you value your leisure time, your peace of mind, and having the conditions in which you can do your job well—you will choose the former. So the school with the lower poverty rate has its pick of the available teachers. One way of changing the equation is by making schools less socioeconomically segregated. But given that the connection of schools to neighborhoods is unavoidable, at least outside of very densely populated areas with good-quality transport systems, and given that desegregating neighborhoods socioeconomically is very slow, even if there is political will to do so, that strategy has limited promise in many areas. Weighting funding formulas so that schools with larger needy populations have more to spend can help to offset other incentives in the labor market. In the United Kingdom this is partially accomplished through a labyrinthine central government funding formula and a "pupil premium" that gives schools with low-income students additional money on a per-pupil basis; the result is that schools with high concentrations of disadvantaged students have up to twice as much funding as schools with affluent populations. Some US states attach (mostly small) weights to socioeconomic disadvantage in their formula for distributing state funds. For example, Delaware grants districts with 30 percent poverty or greater an additional 78 percent per student on top of the standard per pupil amount of state funding; California provides an additional 20 percent for each disadvantaged student, and a further 50 percent per disadvantaged student for districts with high concentrations of disadvantage; Minnesota, Utah, Ohio, New Jersey, South Dakota, Tennessee, Massachusetts, Indiana, and North Carolina all have increments of 10 percent or more. For the most part these measures do not accomplish a great deal more than offset inequalities in locally raised funds that advantage more affluent populations, and they are applied at the district level rather than at the school level (which means that districts are able to respond to local pressure from more affluent parents to spend more on programs for more affluent children in the schools they attend). More radical weightings that would enable schools and districts with high concentrations of disadvantage to compete with other schools for highly effective teachers and school leaders would probably have to be a part of any plan to improve the schools disadvantaged students attend.

CONCLUSION

For the most part I have argued that markets have limited promise for improving education in most circumstances in affluent democracies. It is not that they should be eliminated; that would be impossible and undesirable. Nor am I saying that in specific circumstances some extension of market mechanisms might not be helpful. But markets have many drawbacks, and other reforms promise more. It is true that these other reforms are compatible with some market reforms. But in practice, undue focus by reformers on increased privatization and school choice has distracted political attention from other reforms and has provided some politicians with an excuse not to take pressing issues—such as child poverty, the right kinds of background support for learning, and changes in the teaching career—seriously.

NOTES

1. See Richard Rothstein, *Class and Schools: Using Social, Economic, and Educational Reform to Close the Black-White Achievement Gap* (New York: Teachers College Press, 2004); Richard Rothstein, Rebecca Jacobsen, and Tamara

Wilder, *Grading Education: Getting Accountability Right* (Washington, DC: Economic Policy Institute, 2008); Greg J. Duncan and Richard J. Murnane, *Restoring Opportunity: The Crisis of Inequality and the Challenge for American Education* (Cambridge, MA: Harvard Education Press, 2014).

2. Richard Rothstein, "Whose Problem Is Poverty?," *Educational Leadership* 65, no. 7 (2008): 8.

3. Duncan and Murnane, *Restoring Opportunity*.

4. James J. Heckman, Seong Hyeok Moon, Rodrigo Pinto, Peter A. Savelyev, and Adam Yavitz, "The Rate of Return to the High/Scope Perry Preschool Program," NBER Working Paper 15471, National Bureau of Economic Research, November 2009, http://www.nber.org/papers/w15471.

5. Betty Hart and Todd R. Risley, *Meaningful Differences in the Everyday Experience of Young American Children* (Baltimore: Paul H. Brookes, 1995).

6. Heckman et al., "Rate of Return."

7. David Deming, "Early Childhood Intervention and Life-Cycle Skill Development: Evidence from Head Start," *American Economic Journal: Applied Economics* 1, no. 3 (2009): 111–134.

8. For details on Gautreaux, New Hope, and Moving to Opportunity, see Greg J. Duncan, Aletha C. Huston, and Thomas S. Weisner, *Higher Ground: New Hope for the Working Poor and Their Children* (New York: Russell Sage Foundation, 2007), and Greg J. Duncan and Anita Zuberi, "Mobility Lessons from Gautreaux and Moving to Opportunity," *Northwestern Journal of Law and Social Policy* 1, no. 1 (2006): 110.

9. Joel Klein, Michelle Rhee, et al., "How to Fix Our Schools: A Manifesto by Joel Klein, Michelle Rhee and Other Education Leaders," *Washington Post*, October 10, 2010.

10. Frederick M. Hess, *Common Sense School Reform* (New York: Palgrave Macmillan, 2004), 144–145.

Epilogue

HARRY BRIGHOUSE AND DAVID SCHMIDTZ

WHAT IS IT LIKE FOR friends to strongly disagree about something that really matters to them? In this epilogue, we give our joint reflection on what has come of our debate.

A frustrating feature of some debates about education policy in particular is the assumption that one's opponent is arguing in bad faith. This is not a problem for us. We did not need to debate which of us truly cares about the next generation. We both care. We both know that we both care. We may not have precisely the same hopes for the next generation, but our debate is more about means than ends.

We did not expect to agree on how best to go about leaving a better world for the next generation. But each of us did expect the other to have a highly educated and highly sensible perspective—both on what works and on what is worth wanting. Both of us have spent our careers trying to get the best information we can get about real problems and how best to respond to them. (The previous sentence is not a throwaway line. It identifies both of us as philosophers in a tradition of empiricist realism.)

We could have debated the merits of a polar extreme of complete privatization of all educational services. We could have debated the polar extreme of a government-run and government-funded monopoly on all forms of educational service. We aimed instead to place our discussion within the limits of what it is reasonable to expect in the medium-term future, where the data is, and where a theory has the most straightforwardly testable implication. Testing and evaluating alternatives in comparative terms is not easy and would never be conclusive even in retrospect, because such experiments are never sufficiently well-controlled to count as decisive proof. This does not mean that either of us opts for realism at the expense of ideals. An ideal is not a Platonic abstraction. One way to characterize a realistic ideal is to say it is what is worth aspiring to achieve starting from here. Where can we go from here? Where do we have the most reason to want to go? How much education does a society need? What should we count as success? What should we count as failure? What should we settle for? What lessons can we draw from the experience we have? What matters? What works? How can we build on the success we have already achieved?

Neither of us has a problem with ideal theory insofar as ideal theory is understood as theorizing about ideal responses to the human condition as it really is. However, when it comes time to face the reality of the human condition in a real, situated context—when we ask what an ideal response would be to the challenge of educating the next generation, as that challenge actually manifests itself in our actual world—then one part of coming to grips with reality is understanding how hard it could be to know (or even be reasonably confident about) what an ideal response would be like.

A second part of coming to grips with reality is understanding how two scholars could come to different conclusions without either of them having made a mistake. If two theorists each begin with inevitably incomplete information, they may quite reasonably draw different conclusions. That much is obvious, but then it gets worse. There is a variation on the theme of what psychologists call confirmation bias that is a real problem without exactly being a bias. That is, two identical information processors could process the same two bits of plausible but contradictory information and reach different conclusions, depending on which of those two bits is processed first. Cognition works like this for human beings living in real time: We accept the first bit of information because it is plausible. Later on, we decline to accept the second bit on the grounds that it does not cohere with the first bit, which we have already accepted. If the second bit were overwhelmingly more plausible than the bit that we already believe, then we would change our minds, but the second bit is merely plausible, and "merely plausible" is not enough to change a belief with which we have become comfortable. The problem is not that someone made a mistake but that human beings process information in real time. Our respective backgrounds put us in an excellent position to be just about as objective as human beings can be, while acknowledging that we are all products of our backgrounds and we all process information one bit at a time. So we see things differently. That is to be expected.

We both realize that we cannot simply take successful models and scale them up. There are successful charter school systems. Their elevated performance is driven by an elevated commitment. High-performing charter school systems are a culture. High performance must be cultured with care. We both like charter schools as a modest way of introducing market reforms into public schooling, but we're both aware that what is good about charter schools cannot simply be mass-produced.

Perhaps we disagree somewhat on what is worth wanting for society as a whole. Perhaps we disagree about the role that a system of education can and should play in serving that overall aim for society as a whole. Quite possibly, the role that schools realistically can play has limits no matter what values we're talking about. If equalizing were an overall aim for society as a whole, that would not entail that equalizing is what schools are for. We could argue that regardless of what a community is for, the fact remains that schools are for developing capacities to enable students to flourish as social beings by learning to be of service to their community.

Neither of us rejects the ideal of a society that works more or less to the greatest advantage of the least advantaged. Yet unresolved empirical questions remain regarding whether directing an educational system to promote the greatest advantage of the least advantaged would reliably produce that goal. We might both agree that that is a conceptual possibility without agreeing on how likely that is. Another conceptual possibility is that societies that simply aim to have educational systems that are maximally effective in developing human excellence, wherever the potential may be, are the societies that actually work to the greatest advantage of the least advantaged. It is possible. We may not agree on how likely that is. On the other hand, we do completely agree that if we want to identify neighborhoods where we are most badly failing to develop human potential, it is highly plausible that the poorest neighborhoods are where human potential is most likely to be wasted. It does not take any particular ideological orientation to find that a likely possibility.

Civility and neighborliness (not to mention openness to learning something new) embody a commitment to avoid being too interested in reaching consensus on who has the most important destination. Western civilization's greatest triumph was learning to get past needing to decide which religion is correct, and instead see the question as a matter of jurisdiction: who gets to decide for whom. We would do well to get past secular religion, too.

Whatever the proper aim of a central planner might be in the realm of education, one basic reality check is this: parents *predictably* want something other than what central planners want: parents want a system primarily although obviously not exclusively for the benefit of their own children. Every parent wants their own child to grow up in a society of peace and progress. So, to that extent every parent wants, at least secondarily, much the same as what we both want: namely, a society where every child, including those from the least advantaged homes, grows up with a reasonable aspiration of living a good life.

Central planning faces a problem that can't be wished away: namely, the kind of person who wants power badly enough to do whatever it takes to win it, even in a democracy, is not like the rest of us. Power-seekers have their own agendas in addition to whatever ideals they espouse, although in democracies the need to campaign drives them to *talk* as if their agenda were just like ours. There is no real solution so far as we know: the fact that power corrupts is baked into the human condition. There are better and worse ways of coping or failing to cope with that problem. But when we ignore the problem in any realm, including education, and imagine that we can trust those who would centralize the planning of it, we thereby enable power-seekers who end up making the problem worse. The difference in our approaches to how schooling should be provided and regulated reflects, in part, different strategic orientations to the problems of central planning.

INDEX

For the benefit of digital users, indexed terms that span two pages (e.g., 52–53) may, on occasion, appear on only one of those pages.